# SWEET BABY

# SWEET BABY

## *HOW TO SOOTHE YOUR NEWBORN*

# Marc Weissbluth, M.D.

## Acknowledgments

I am grateful to those parents who read the manuscript of *Crybabies* and Barbara Bernstein who contributed to the writing and editing of *Crybabies* which was published in 1984. *Crybabies* inspired me to write *Sweet Baby.* Special thanks to Mrs. BernadetteTramm and Mrs. Sharon Fiffer.

To order:
Phone: 312-642-5515 Extension 9234
www.SweetBabies.com

ISBN: 0-9666140-1-1

# TABLE OF CONTENTS

*This book is dedicated to*
**Linda, Daniel, Michael, Jed,** *and* **Elliot**
*Who taught me how to love children.*

# INTRODUCTION

Birthing a baby unleashes unique and powerful forces within the mother and the baby. The experience of child-birth is an event unlike all others. The joy of having a baby is different from the more ordinary pleasures women experi-ence. Caressing her, holding her warm skin to your cheek, feeding her, gazing into her eyes . . . your heart melts. Could there be a more beautiful and graceful creation?

During the first few days, your child appears so peaceful and so calm that you may wonder if you have to wake her to feed her. You may notice that she does not suck with very much strength or interest before she snoozes off into deep slumber. It is normal for your baby to lose weight during these first few days. If your baby was born early, this quiet and sleepy state may last longer than a few days.

After a few days of age, or around the due date for babies born early, things begin to change. Your baby becomes more wakeful, alert, and sucks with more strength. She has a more wide open-eyed look. It's as if the sleepy brain starts to wake up, just in time to catch the breast milk if you are nursing your baby. The weight loss slowly stops and she starts to rapidly regain her birth weight and more.

As your baby becomes more wakeful, she moves her arms

and legs around more, her eyes study you more and follow you about, and sometimes she seems to fuss for several minutes. To 'Fuss' is to become upset, to fret, to be less settled, or to get stirred up. During the fussy spell, your baby appears nervous, agitated, and unable to fall asleep or stay asleep. Sometimes she appears 'Irritable.' When irritable, she may be very excitable, easily upset, and unhappily sensitive to stimuli such as loud noises and she may easily melt down into a crying state if not soothed by her parents. It is not clear what is annoying or exasperating her. This behavior also 'irritates' both mother and father. Parents feel sympathy for their baby and displeasure that she requires so much more attention. When extra soothing seems to not help much, she may provoke in you feelings of impatience or anger.

All babies have moments of fussiness and irritability. Some babies have so much of this fussiness and irritability that if you added up all the minutes of fussiness and irritability in a day, it would be more than three hours each day. If your baby behaves this way for more than three days a week and for more than three weeks, then it is called 'Extreme Fussiness.' The word 'colic' has been used to describe babies with extreme fussiness but there is no reason to give them a separate label. I prefer to use the term 'extreme fussiness' because babies fuss much more than they cry. Nevertheless, some babies with extreme fussiness also have moments of inconsolable crying. This means that she might cry despite your efforts to comfort her.

This book will explain how to soothe all babies during their fussy moments.

Every new parent quickly discovers two new facts: It's not always easy to soothe your baby and you can't send your fussy baby back.

But admit it, there are times when you wish you could. If your baby has extreme fussiness, he is putting you through a trying and confusing time. You may face hours of fussing or crying every day. You may feel that your baby is beyond your reach. You may not be getting much rest. You may feel guilty, angry, or just unlucky. You may not really understand what is happening, or why.

This book is for you.

## *My First Experience with Extreme Fussiness*

I was a medical student when my first son was born. He fussed and cried for hours on end. Neither my wife nor I thought this was strange. We assumed that all babies behaved this way. No one told us, fortunately, that he had a "condition." We didn't know enough to worry that it might be because he was a boy, or our firstborn, or breast-fed, or that we were unwittingly making him miserable. Maybe the complete absence of teaching about extreme fussiness in medical school was a blessing for us.

I remember rocking my son for hours on end while trying to memorize neuroanatomy. I would sometimes pretend to close my eyes, hoping he would do the same, but every time I peeked, he had his radar-beam gaze fixed on me. Calming him down always took an hour or two of rocking. Once he began breathing deeply and regularly in my arms I could put him down in his crib. But if I was impatient and tried to put him down before this deep sleep developed, he would arch his back, open his eyes wide, and start to fuss and cry once again.

My wife was studying Dostoyevsky or Old Church Slavonic, which is harder than neuroanatomy. We took turns pacing, walking, and rocking. In our student apartment, my son's room was above the postage stamp-sized kitchen. I remember unwashed dinner dishes piled up late into the night because the slightest banging would awaken our little angel. Looking back, I think we were too tired and preoccupied with our studies to worry much about his behavior. But I have never felt the same about neuroanatomy.

If this routine sounds familiar to you, you might like to know that things settled down for us within a few months. Our son became a delightful baby. Our three subsequent children had no excessive fussing or crying. I most likely would not even remember those first noisy months had I not developed a special interest, as a pediatrician and researcher, in extreme fussiness and how babies can be soothed.

Extreme fussiness is what that was, although I didn't call it that at the time. There is some question about whether giving a label to a pattern of behavior like this makes it seems better or worse. Some parents are relieved to know that this kind of fussing is so common that it's called something. Others feel that, as one mother told me, "Once you give it a name, it's a real problem." A father was perfectly willing to admit that his young daughter fussed and screamed for hours on end, but emphatically denied that she could have extreme fussiness. If parents would rather think they just have a very fussy baby, this is fine. For, as we shall see, the line between the normal fussing behavior and 'extreme fussiness' is an arbitrary one. When does sadness become depression? When does overweight become obesity? When does intelligence become genius? Fussing and crying becomes extreme fussiness when the researchers doing the defining say it does.

All babies fuss some of the time and most parents are not sure how to handle it. This book will tell you how to soothe your baby. You will be better able to soothe your baby if you understand what is known about fussy babies and extreme fussiness.

# I

## WHY DOES MY BABY FUSS?

# 1

## Why Does My Baby Fuss & What Is Extreme Fussiness?

Extreme fussiness/colic in infants is characterized by spells or paroxysmal attacks of irritability, fussing, or crying occurring in the evening hours in babies who are healthy. Traditional research focused on extreme crying (colic) because that was the major complaint of parents and the most dramatic observable feature. Contemporary research has focused on fussiness for two reasons: fussing occurs twice as much as crying and it is possible that successful management of fussiness may prevent fussing escalating into colic. Traditional views regarding extreme fussiness have been based on data obtained almost exclusively by a reliance on reports from parents. Obviously, parental anxiety, fatigue, and preconceptions may influence their descriptions of their infants' behavior. Contemporary views of extreme fussiness have included objective data derived from voice-activated audio recordings and observations in the child's home. Results from these contemporary studies are compatible with traditional observations but an interesting question is now raised: *Can a baby who does not cry much have extreme fussiness/colic?*

The traditional view was developed by a famous British pediatrician, Illingworth, who defined colic as "violent rhythmical, screaming attacks which did not stop when the infants were picked up, and for which no cause, such as underfeeding, could be found." Wessel, an American pediatrician, diagnosed a colicky infant as "one who, otherwise healthy and well-fed, had paroxysms of irritability, fussing or crying lasting for a total of more than 3 hours a day and occurring on more than 3 days in one week . . . and that the paroxysms continued to recur for more than 3 weeks." Thus, the definition of colic usually includes the elements of *long durations of irritability, fussing, or crying per day, occurring many days per week, and continuing for many weeks* in a healthy infant.

Their results showed that the attacks do not usually occur during the first few days but are present in about 80% of affected infants by 2 weeks of age. All affected infants have the onset of their spells by 3 weeks of age. About 80% of extremely fussy infants begin their spells between 5 P.M. and 8 P.M., and their spells usually end by midnight. An additional 12% of infants experience their spells later in the evening, starting between 7 P.M. and 10 P.M. and ending by 2 A.M. At 2 months of age, about 50% of extremely fussy infants no longer have these crying spells, and by 3 months of age, an additional 30% of infants are free of fussiness. By about 4 months of age, an additional 10%, or 90% of all previously extremely fussy/colicky infants, are free of symptoms. The average duration of the fussy spell lasts almost 4 hours. The onset of extreme fussiness in premature infants is usually delayed and starts near the expected date of delivery regardless of the gestational age at birth.

Extreme fussy spells are *not* qualitatively different from normal fussing but differ from fussing only in intensity, duration, or persistence. Again, there are differences in quantity but not quality. The documented natural history of normal fussing regarding its onset, time of occurrence, and cessation parallels that of extreme fussiness. Extreme fussiness represents only an extreme form of normally occurring infant behaviors.

During spells of extreme fussiness, the baby is often described as hypertonic because the entire body is stiffened, the fists are tightly clenched, and the legs are flexed rigidly over the abdomen. The babies sometimes have uncoordinated jerky movements of their limbs described as batting or flapping of the arms or kicking the legs. At other times the movements are described as writhing, twisting, or turning. These movements are not present at other times, and these babies have normal neurologic examinations.

Air swallowing occurs during these agitated movements and during the crying spells, and this swallowed air is probably the explanation for the gassiness that is another feature of extremely fussy babies. There is no evidence to suggest that the gassiness in extremely fussy babies is caused by disease of the gastrointestinal system. There is also no strong evidence linking extreme fussiness with the method of feeding or food allergy.

Another feature of some, but not all, extremely fussy infants is stimulus sensitivity; they appear to be either easily startled or easily awakened. Frequent awakenings at night often occur in these infants. A bothersome feature of colicky infants in general is extreme daytime wakefulness manifested by brief naps or no naps.

When thinking about fussiness from a modern view, it is important to note that Wessel's research focused on paroxysmal *fussing*, not crying. Wessel's definition of extreme fussiness/colic did *not* require that a baby must cry a great deal; extreme fussiness is compatible with Wessel's definition. In fact, recent research has established that fussing is a behavior that occurs more frequently and lasts longer than crying.

Ian St James-Roberts defined *fussing* as when the baby is unsettled and irritable and may be vocalizing but not continuously crying. *Crying* was defined as periods of intense distressed vocalization. *Extreme fussiness/colic* was defined as inconsolable crying plus other behavior, perhaps due to stomach or bowel pain. He collected data from parent diaries, 24-hour voice activated audio recordings, and home visits. Overall, babies exhibited about 171 minutes of fuss, cry, or colic behavior each day and the distribution was approximately 60% fussing, 30% crying, and 10% colic. In other words, on any given day, fussing occurs twice as much as crying. The actual amount of time for extreme fussiness/colic was only about 14 minutes!

Out of the entire group, he isolated a subgroup whom he called persistent criers (these were extremely fussy/colicky babies) based upon having 3 or more hours of fussing or crying per day. In this group of persistent criers, 221 minutes of fuss, cry, or extreme fussiness/colic occurred every day but again, only 11% or 25 minutes was colic compared to 61% fuss and 28% cry behavior. As before, in this smaller but more bothersome group, babies fussed twice as much as they cried.

In fact, of these persistent criers, 63% never had a single episode of extreme fussiness/colic! In other words, they were always consolable. Although they did fuss and cry a great deal throughout the day, for 3 or more hours, maybe their mothers behaved somewhat like African !Kung San mothers to prevent inconsolable crying.

The author concluded that low intensity fussing was much more common than intense crying and that fuss, cry, and colic form a single continuum. They are not separate behaviors.

Extreme fussiness is a puzzle, and I do not claim to have solved it. This is not the sort of book that has a story to sell. You will find no sweeping theories, startling discoveries, or three-step solutions. You will find a summary of everything that is known or believed about extreme fussiness right now. I believe that the more you know about extreme fussiness, the less worried you will be.

Now you have read some definitions of extreme fussiness and may decide that your baby is like this. Because extreme fussiness is different things to different people, and because factual information has been scarce and inconclusive, many "explanations" have evolved through the years. Even doctors and nurses repeat some of them as fact. Totally ineffectual treatments are often recommended. One of my purposes here is to separate myth from fact. I will be examining the most common old wives' tales about extreme fussiness, the ones your parents have probably already heard from helpful relatives and friends. Then I will review what we actually know about extreme fussiness, based on properly conducted experiments reported in professional journals.

I will offer suggestions on coping with extreme fussiness which have helped hundreds of my patients. I will talk about preventing extreme fussiness from turning into a long-term behavioral sleeping problem, and how to solve that problem if it occurs.

I will also offer some intriguing new theories on extreme fussiness. In the past few years, a number of studies have pointed to links connecting extreme fussiness; a certain kind of infant temperament, sleep habits, and such body functions as control of breathing during sleep. I have brought together here a number of studies that shed light on the extreme fussiness/colic mystery. It does not make a tidy package yet—there is much work to do—but I feel the answer to the extreme fussiness mystery lies in this direction.

### Defining the Condition Called Extreme Fussiness/Colic

Some doctors maintain that extreme fussiness, by definition, must involve spells of violent, rhythmical screaming. Other doctors say it is not extreme fussiness unless the baby's legs are drawn up and he seems to expel gas. Some doctors use the timing of the condition—the way the spells usually start about two weeks of age, end around three months, and are worst in the evening—as the indication of extreme fussiness. A few researchers claim that only babies who are ill tempered and fussy all their waking hours can be called extremely fussiness. On the other hand, one of the earliest students of extreme fussiness wrote, "The outstanding impression given by the extremely fussy baby, except in the evening, is that he is a well, thriving, well-fed and well-managed baby with nothing wrong with him."

So let us use a broad definition. This book, when it uses the term "extreme fussiness/colic" means: irritability, fussiness, or crying for which no physical cause can be found, which lasts more than three hours a day, occurs more than three days a week and continues for more than three weeks. Often, some of the crying is inconsolable.

Let's examine this definition point by point.

"Inconsolable crying." This is probably the aspect of extreme fussiness that distresses parents most. Most young infants can be quieted with holding, walking, a pacifier, a car ride, a feeding, quiet talking, and so forth. Extremely fussiness babies, by contrast, are sometimes simply beyond help. Parental intervention seems to have no effect, or only a temporary one. That extremely fussiness babies cannot be consoled is a significant factor that, as we will see later, offers some clues to the nature of extreme fussiness.

"No physical cause." Extreme fussiness occurs only among healthy infants. If there is a medical problem that might be causing the baby discomfort, her crying is not extreme fussiness and, of course, she needs medical attention. If something in her environment—temperature, noise, or wet diapers, — is causing her to cry, it is easily corrected.

"More than three hours a day." This is an arbitrary figure. In itself, three hours of fussing in one day is not unusual. Only if it happens repeatedly might it indicate extreme fussiness.

"More than three days a week." Most extremely fussiness babies have good days when they hardly cry at all, sleep through the night, and seem to be "over it." Parents are doubly upset when the fussing starts again. In my experience, extreme fussiness wanes and returns. Almost never does it follow the same pattern day after day.

"More than three weeks." Extreme fussiness is a persistent condition. This does not mean that you must endure three weeks of screaming before you seek help. Just remember that an occasional bad night, even a bad week, is not unusual.

Table 1 fleshes out this definition of extreme fussiness somewhat.

*Table 1*

# DESCRIPTIONS OF
# EXTREME FUSSINESS

*EXTREMELY FUSSY INFANTS HAVE SPELLS OF:*

Unexplained fussiness, fretfulness, irritability, crying
Piercing screaming attacks
Explosive or inconsolable crying
Noise and rumbling in the gut, excessive flatulence or gas
(and/or) apparent abdominal pain with legs drawn up onto
the abdomen
Fists clenched

*EXTREMELY FUSSY INFANTS ARE:*

Vigorous
Intense, wound up
Energetic, excitable
Easily startled
Gassy
Grimacing, stiffening, twisting
Easily and frequently awakened
"Squirmy as a worm in hot ashes"

## *Is Extreme Fussiness a Disease?*

Babies do fuss but they don't 'have' fussiness like you
might 'have' a disease. Fussing is to infants what adolescence
is to teen-agers. Adolescence is not a disease. Fussy infants
and rebellious adolescents are difficult for parents to deal
with but these behaviors are related to stages of development, not a medical problem. The problem with thinking
that extreme fussiness is a medical problem is that unnecessary 'treatments' are given hoping for a 'cure.' Thinking that
something is medically wrong with your newborn casts a
shadow over becoming a parent. All babies outgrow fussiness.

There are degrees of fussiness. You may have seen a pop-

ular child-care book, which has a chart showing extreme
fussiness/colic behavior in one column, just plain crying in
another. It is supposed to help parents determine if their
child has extreme fussiness or not. This is misleading. Extreme fussiness is not an absolute, all-or-nothing proposi-
tion. In fact, one researcher, Dr. Joseph Brennemann, wrote
that fussiness is "an almost inevitable occurrence sometime
in early infancy. Few infants escape it." He is right that all babies have periods of unexplained fussiness. The fussiness that
drives parents to distraction and puzzles pediatricians, the
condition that I think deserves the name "extreme fussiness"
is that which lasts for several hours a day over the course of
several weeks or months. Brennemann does remind us that
extreme fussiness is not some freak condition set apart from
normal infant behavior. It is an extreme form of what all babies do. *Extreme fussiness is not a disease.*

### Extreme fussiness Is Very Common

If your baby has extreme fussiness, you are not alone.
Once you begin talking and asking about it, you will be
amazed at the company you are in. Ask your parents, in-
laws, aunts and uncles. I guarantee, yours is not the first extremely fussy baby in your family (although extreme
fussiness is not hereditary). Talk to your friends, and you'll
find that yours is far from being the only extreme fussy baby
in your neighborhood.

One out of five babies has extreme fussiness. It occurs in
all cultures. The Chinese describe what we call extreme fussiness as "hundred-days-crying," and consider it a normal behavior pattern. The Vietnamese call it "Three months plus
ten days crying". The Koreans have a "One Hundred Day
Celebration" and the Japanese call it "Evening Crying." The
Asian view is that fussiness is a normal stage of development through which all children pass. That used to be a common view in the West before doctors made it into a medical
problem involving the colon (from which the word 'colic' is
derived). Remember that this condition has been recorded

for hundreds of years. For example, Shakespeare's lines about the seven ages of man: "At first, *the infant crying* and puking in the nurse's arms."

The first pediatrics textbook in English, The Boke of Chyldren, refers to "colicke" as "rumbling in the gut." This was in 1553, before the introduction of coffee and tobacco to England (so much for blaming the mother's bad habits for her child's distress). Do not think that our hectic lifestyle is responsible for extreme fussiness. Extreme fussiness has been with us as long as there have been babies, and we are only now beginning to understand what it's all about.

*Never Forget Four Important Things About Extreme Fussiness*

1. Your baby is healthy and will thrive.
2. You are not the cause of your baby's extreme fussiness; it's not your fault.
3. It will pass.
4. You can take steps to cope with extreme fussiness and to make sure that there are no lasting ill effects.

# 2

# Doctors and Extreme Fussiness

If extreme fussiness is so common, why doesn't it get more publicity? Judging from the dearth of information on extreme fussiness, you would never guess that it affects over 20 percent of all babies born. You are not alone; over seven hundred thousand infants each year in the United States behave this way. This is the first book, which fully discusses the extreme fussiness mystery and how to soothe your baby.

I have consulted with many parents of extremely fussy infants. They have helped me see that extreme fussiness is one of the "dirty little secrets" of pediatrics. Often, parents are made to feel embarrassed about mentioning it. Many pediatricians don't want to hear about it. Your own pediatrician may have said, "Oh, that's just a touch of extreme fussiness," and left you to cope on your own. Try to understand the reasons for this lack of professional advice.

## The Curious History of Extreme Fussiness

Historically, extreme fussiness has eluded medical understanding. At various times, researchers have blamed extreme fussiness on: overfeeding; underfeeding; food with too much carbohydrate, too much starch, too much protein;

"allergy": a reaction to horsehair, feathers, orange juice; overpermissive parents; too much picking up of the baby; exposure to cold; lack of oral satisfaction, among other causes. Mostly, because it was incorrectly thought to be a medical "problem" instead of a stage of development, claims for discovering "cures" have often been only wishful thinking.

Suggested "cures" have included: weaning the baby from the breast; adding goat's milk, olive oil, or banana powder to her diet; treatment with bicarbonate of soda, chloral hydrate, opium derivatives, peppermint, or dill water; giving an enema or suppository; offering a pacifier; handling the baby more gently; and a drink of whiskey. (Illingworth clarifies "taken by the baby.")

I do not want you to think this is unusual. Reviewing the literature on almost any condition gives you a variety of absurd notions that were taken seriously for a time. In the case of extreme fussiness, however, since a cause has not been isolated nor a definition agreed upon, so many of these mistaken ideas have hung on. Only in the last thirty years have controlled experiments comparing groups of extremely fussy and more garden-variety fussy babies been performed.

### Extreme Fussiness Is Not the Sort of Problem Doctors Like

Little is taught about extreme fussiness in medical schools. It is not the sort of problem doctors feel comfortable with. It is not a disease. It does not have a definite cause. It does not even have a telltale set of symptoms. Nothing about extreme fussiness shows up on x-rays, stool analyses, blood tests. Diagnosis is subjective. There is no treatment of choice, which, understandably, makes doctors shy away from it.

One thing pediatricians do know about extreme fussiness is that it does not kill or harm infants. They know that the infants will outgrow the behavior fairly quickly. What they do not realize is how devastating it is to the parents while it is going on. The physician will frequently say to the mother, "This is not serious. If only you would relax and take it easy, then your baby would calm down." Yet I have given talks on extreme fussiness to groups of physicians and played for them a tape of an extremely fussy baby crying. After no more than a minute and a half of this noise, I get cries from the audience: "Enough!" "Turn it off!" Perhaps if pediatricians had to spend even one evening with an extremely fussy patient, they would be more sympathetic.

### The Nature Of Extreme Fussiness In Behavioral Research

Another reason for the neglect of extreme fussiness may lie with the nature of research into human behavior. Some doctors and researchers like to observe children only when awake, while others like to study children asleep. Like larks and owls, these professionals do not flock together— they do not talk to each other or share their findings. Extreme fussiness, which is a strange sort of condition somewhere between awake and asleep behavior, has fallen in an academic no-man's-land.

There is also a species of researchers I call hawks. Rather than observe, they like to do things to babies and then measure their responses. They snap rubber bands against heels, block the airflow through the nose, and make a baby breathe a low oxygen air-gas mixture. Some of these hawks seem truly aggressive; however, they have added greatly to our knowledge of child development. Unfortunately, there is no way for them to provoke or simulate an extreme fussy spell in the laboratory. Few researchers care to be out taking measurements in the evening, when most extreme fussiness occurs. Since every baby is different, and no baby's extreme fussiness is exactly the same from day to day, controlled experiments are difficult. This is why extreme fussiness has been described by the larks, but only recently really studied by the owls and hawks.

In the academic aviary, larks, owls, and hawks live in different tress. These various professionals have their own journals and their own languages. Specific kinds of behaviors are usually studied separately from one another: crying is studied separately from social smiling, night awakenings are studied separately from length of night sleep periods. Yet extreme fussiness involves many kinds of behaviors. My intent is to explain, in plain English, how seemingly separate infant behaviors might relate to each other: extreme fussiness, crying, temperament, and sleeping problems. Extreme fussiness has not fallen into any discipline's territory so far, but now it may well be in a territory of it own!

### A Bias Against Moms?

I believe there is also an element of condescension towards women deriving from the time when most pediatricians were males. When some male physicians see a distraught, tearful, exhausted mother asking for help with her child's extreme fussiness, they tend to assume the problem lies with her. Even if they admit extreme fussiness is a pediatric problem, they take an easy out: blame the mother; blame her diet, breast milk, choice of formula, inexperience, her overly active imagination, and so on. In this sense, extreme fussiness is a little like menstrual cramps: male doctors who've never experienced them used to trivialize this pain and assumed it is all in the woman's head.

Some doctors are so unwilling to talk seriously about extreme fussiness that the mother resolves never to bring it up again. Her baby may still fuss or cry, but as far as the doctor knows the condition has abated. So the doctors who scoff most at reports of extreme fussiness often have their mistaken ideas confirmed. Needless to say, you shouldn't pretend to your pediatrician that your baby's extreme fussiness has gone away it if hasn't. You will be helping him perpetuate his ignorance, and your stress.

### What Can a Doctor Do About Extreme fussiness?

As far as treatment goes, most pediatricians do not believe there is anything they can do. They try to stall and/or reassure the mother until the extreme fussiness runs its natural course. Some try to treat extreme fussiness with phenobarbital, herbal teas, or drugs intended to prevent gas formation in the stomach. Even antacids have been used! Other drugs, which decrease the muscle tone in the intestines, have been prescribed. The decision whether to prescribe drugs depends on the pediatrician's training, whether he or she had children with extreme fussiness, and the amount of pressure the doctor is getting from the parents to try to stop the screaming.

I am frequently amused when a pediatrician announces that he has "cured" a case of extreme fussiness. Usually he has had the mother try a series of "treatments" over the course of several months. Then around the child's twelve- or sixteen-week birthday, one treatment has magically worked. Alas, that treatment doesn't work on the next child, or the next, or the next. The point is that the extreme fussiness cured itself, and would have done so in any event. Mistakenly attributing the cure of extreme fussiness to the last week's treatment has led to no end of unhelpful ideas about how to cure extreme fussiness. This often happens with conditions that clear up spontaneously. Your doctor may suggest chicken soup for a cold and you may find that after eating chicken soup for six days your cold is gone, but that does not mean the chicken soup cured your cold.

Doctors can keep parents from exhausting themselves physically and emotionally over mythical causes and cures. Doctors can offer a sympathetic ear, calm understanding, and sincere interest. A follow-up telephone call to parents asking, "How did things go last night" can be an invaluable boost to their morale. A doctor should see the mother in person often enough to look for signs of exhaustion, despair or great family stress, and be prepared to recommend help.

### You and Your Pediatrician

Do not lose faith in your pediatrician if he or she seems at a loss over your extremely fussy baby. This is a tricky problem, which some physicians handle better than others. Your doctor may be splendid about every other aspect of your child's health and development. You may be lucky enough to fine someone else—a sympathetic relative, a friend who has been through extreme fussiness herself, a clinic nurse—to help you through this time. However, if your baby's extreme fussiness makes your pediatrician impatient, patronizing, or less willing to spend time with you, this may be as good a time as any to find a more sympathetic doctor. Don't simply accept your pediatrician's suggestions regarding switching formulas or hospitalization. If such advice is given, ask your baby's doctor: What do you really expect to accomplish by this treatment?

# 3

## Eleven Myths About Extreme Fussiness (and Why You Shouldn't Believe Them)

Once friends and relatives hear (or decide) that you have a baby with extreme fussiness, the advice will start. You will hear all sorts of theories about the causes of extreme fussiness. People will offer their own pet remedies, and you will probably become very confused.

Here are eleven popular fallacies about extreme fussiness. They have grown up and gained acceptance partly because extreme fussiness may mean different things to different people. Since there is no universally accepted definition, the field is wide open. Some of these fallacies are based on observed relationships, one-time coincidences, or simply what seems logical. None of them can stand up to scientific scrutiny. I will explain why you should not believe any of them. Then I hope you will put them out of your mind and devote your energy to coping with your noisy little bundle.

*Fallacy #1: There Is No Such Thing as Extreme Fussiness.*

Some doctors say they have never seen an extremely fussy baby. They believe the problem is with overanxious, inexperienced mothers who exaggerate normal fussing and crying all out of proportion. I would remind these doctors that they seldom see babies in the evening, when extreme fussiness is usually at its worst. They do not have to listen to hours of crying day after day. Too many mothers—experienced, calm, third- and fourth-time mothers—have reported similar crying patterns for extreme fussiness to be a fiction.

*Fallacy #2: Maternal Anxiety Causes Extreme Fussiness.*

No more destructive a belief could be imagined than this one. Imagine telling a mother who is already worried about her child's crying that she is responsible! The guilt, resentment, anger and frustration produced by this fallacy is enormous. It can cause others in the household to blame the mother for the extreme fussiness. Worse, it can cause the mother to believe it herself.

Believing that extreme fussiness might be her fault can keep a mother from getting the help she needs. Once she decides that she is less than perfect at mothering, discussing the infant's behavior with her pediatrician or with anybody becomes painful.

If a parent believes it is her or his fault that the baby is miserable, every cry becomes an accusation. It is likely that extreme fussiness—and the fallacy that parental inadequacy has caused it—is sometimes related to child abuse or other domestic violence. One abusive father I know was untroubled by what he felt was "hunger crying," but became violent at the sound of extreme fussiness crying, which he interpreted as disapproval. "The baby was angry at me," he said, and he reacted by striking the infant.

As you will read in the next chapter, careful studies have shown that mothers of extremely fussy babies are no more anxious, high-strung, or emotionally unstable than the mothers of quiet babies. Parents are not responsible for extreme fussiness.

*Fallacy #3: Extreme Fussiness Is A Gastrointestinal Problem.*

This may be the most deeply entrenched myth about extreme fussiness. The term "colic" itself comes from "colon" implying some connection with the digestive system. The first English language book on pediatrics, The Boke of Chyldren, published over four hundred years ago, described extreme fussiness as noise and 'peine' in the gut.

It's not hard to understand where this idea came from. Often in the course of fussing and crying spells, infants draw their legs up to their abdomens and pass gas. Spells of extreme fussiness often occur after meals, suggesting something amiss with digestion. Also, extreme fussiness and crying has been described as waxing and waning, as if waves of colonic spasms were afflicting the infant. The smooth muscle in the colon does in fact contract in regular waves, thus pushing food and fecal matter through. Thus, observers through the centuries have made the connection: extreme fussiness originates in the abdomen. But, as you will read in the next chapter, older researchers have tried to prove this theory and come up empty-handed. Illingworth and Jorup were two researchers who used x-rays and barium enemas, and found no special gastrointestinal activity during extreme fussiness spells.

The extreme fussiness behavior which gave rise to this theory—in the drawing up of legs, turning red, clenching fists—also occurs, momentarily, whenever an infant gets a baby shot. So it may not indicate pain in the abdomen at all—it may simply be the way a young infant expresses discomfort, from whatever location. As for the gas, I believe that as she cries, an infant swallows air that must be expelled. It is a result, not a cause, of prolonged crying. Similarly, the waxing and waning feature is probably the way any baby would cry who has been at it for hours.

Most convincing is this: extremely fussy babies do not have any symptoms of intestinal disorders. No poor weight gain, no excessive spitting or vomiting, no constipation or diarrhea, and no need for extra feedings. Surely, after all these years of careful study, some physical corroboration for this idea should have shown up. Therefore, there is no reason to believe that extreme fussiness reflects a gastrointestinal problem.

On the other hand, newer research, performed by my wife, suggests that there may be a normally occurring chemical imbalance that develops in many babies causing contractions of the smooth muscle lining the gut. More about this later.

### Fallacy #4: Something the Baby Has Eaten Disagrees with Her.

If you have a food allergy, you might assume that your extremely fussy baby does too. It is true that some children are allergic to the cow's milk protein in some formulas, but this is very uncommon. Allergy to cow's milk protein usually causes bloody diarrhea. Nevertheless, a common treatment for extreme fussiness is switching formulas from those containing cow's milk protein to those derived from goat's milk or soybean protein, or some "hypoallergenic" formulas.

One published report claimed to prove that cow's milk protein in infant formulas caused extreme fussiness. However, serious errors in that study invalidated the authors' conclusions. For example, there was no randomization in the placement of infants into different study groups. The parents were not "blind" or unaware of the changes in the type of formula, which they were giving their infants. The investigators never defined what they meant by a "cure." And although they claimed that these extremely fussy infants were allergic to cow's milk, about 50 percent of these so-called allergic babies failed to show symptoms when given cow's milk at three or six months of age! The authors claimed they had "outgrown" the allergy, when in fact they had outgrown the extreme fussiness.

Those same authors also claimed that when a nursing mother has cow's milk in her diet, the cow's milk protein gets into her breast milk, causing extreme fussiness in her baby. This study also had serious flaws, for example, the results were based on only ten infants.

The truth is that there is no well-designed study that shows that the diet of nursing mothers has anything to do with extreme fussiness.

In fact, a careful, objective study done in 1981 by Dr. William Liebman at the University of California School of Medicine concluded that cow's milk protein allergy has no significant role in causing infant extreme fussiness.

A related fallacy is that "allergy" in general causes extreme fussiness. This dates from a period when allergies had just been discovered and were used as the explanation for nearly every medical problem. This vague concept has no basis in fact and is probably only a smokescreen to hide our lack of information.

Another food-related extreme fussiness theory is lactose intolerance. Lactose, commonly known as milk sugar, is present in all commercial formulas that contain cow's milk. About 10 percent of white Americans, and a much higher percentage of blacks, suffer from intolerance to lactose. It may cause abdominal pain, gassiness, and diarrhea, but does it cause extreme fussiness? Liebman's study evaluated extremely fussy infants for lactose intolerance. He concluded that it does not have a significant role in causing extreme fussiness. Therefore, prescribing lactose-free formulas or having nursing mothers stop drinking milk simply does not make sense.

Researchers who believe that cow's milk protein allergy or lactose intolerance causes extreme fussiness have never explained how these offending foods, which are ingested throughout the day, would trigger attacks of fussiness only at a particular time: the vast majority of infants with extreme fussiness suffer their worst spells in the evening hours.

As you can see, the strategy of switching to formulas which are free of cow's milk protein and lactose, such as protein derived from soybeans, makes no sense in the treatment of extreme fussiness. However, there are enough different brands of formulas so that a pediatrician might suggest a formula switch each week with the idea of buying time until the infant outgrows the extreme fussiness. This is a deplorable strategy, especially when the doctor should know it would not work. He might think that the parent would feel better if she has something different to try, but, on the contrary, I suspect that this only increases the mother's frustration. As each successive new formula fails (until the infant is about three months old!), she suspects more and more that something must be dreadfully wrong with her child or with herself.

If your physician suggests switching formulas in an attempt to cure your baby's extreme fussiness, do not lose patience. Remember that this is a long-standing practice. Ask you pediatrician to discuss frankly whether he or she thinks the treatment will really work, or whether it is designed simply to placate you so that you can feel better.

### *Fallacy #5: The Nursing Mother's Diet.*

Foods that cause stomach upset or gas in the nursing mother go on to cause extreme fussiness in her baby, right? Wrong! This fanciful notion is contrary to everything we know about how digestion occurs.

This makes as much sense as saying that if you eat chocolate, you will make chocolate milk.

Here are the facts. The foods eaten by the mother get broken down into simple elemental foodstuffs and absorbed by her digestive system. Breast milk is made from these absorbed nutrients. By contrast, gas in the mother's intestine is formed much further along in the process by the action of naturally occurring bacteria in food the mother has eaten. It is impossible that gas in the mother's colon, derived from eating something like beans or cabbage, could get into her breast milk. Yet some nursing mothers report that eliminating certain foods from their own diets improved their chil-

dren's behavior. You may have heard some of your friends
swear this is true, but it is not. It is only coincidence, or wishful thinking.

Mothers who believe that their breast milk is causing their
children's misery must be reassured that it is not, since it may
cause mothers to stop nursing when there is no reason to do
so. Since nursing is one of the few things that can sometimes
soothe a fussing baby, a mother can be filled with conflicts
over whether it helps or hurts.

A professional woman torn between staying home to
nurse and returning to work sometimes uses her baby's fussiness to resolve the conflict between staying at home or returning to work. She may say to herself, "Since I decided to
stay home to nurse my baby, but my breast milk disagrees
with him, I might as well go back to work and let someone
else give him formula." A mother should not use the belief
that "bad" or insufficient breast milk causes fussiness as a
reason to return to work quickly; it may provide a handy excuse, but it has no basis in fact.

You'll read some practical tips on breastfeeding an extremely fussy baby in Chapter 9. In the meantime, you can be
sure that "bad" or insufficient milk has nothing to do with
extreme fussiness.

### *Fallacy #6: Breastfed Babies Have Less Extreme Fussiness.*

Since there is a prevalent assumption that breastfed
infants are healthier in all regards, there also is the assumption that breastfed infants are protected against extreme
fussiness. However, several studies have shown that extreme
fussiness occurs as often for breastfed infants as for bottle-
fed infants. Dr. T.C. Boulton's study from the University of
Adelaide in 1979 noted that extreme fussiness was unusually
common in Australia (40 percent of all babies), but that it
was as common among breastfed as formula-fed infants
were.

Fussiness has been studied among tribes such as the

!Kung San where the mothers practice continuous care and contact: the baby is always in contact with the mother, the baby is always carried or held upright by the mother, the baby sleeps with his mother, the mother responds to every fussy sound immediately no matter how quiet the fret is, and they are breast fed about four times an hour. Just like American babies, these babies have a similar pattern of increasing fussiness peaking during the second month of life and then decreasing. This strongly suggests that the universal pattern of increasing then decreasing fussiness has a biologic basis independent of style of parenting.

However, although the !Kung San babies cried as often as American babies, the duration of crying for each bout of crying was shorter. This suggests the possibility of changes in caretaking might decrease the total amount of fussiness/crying. But the behavior of !Kung San is different from American mothers in so many ways, it would be false to conclude that breast feeding alone prevents fussiness.

*Fallacy #7: Firstborn Children Have Extreme Fussiness More Often.*

Many mothers swear this is so, but why? Firstborn children are a little like a trial cake. Probably out of uncertainty and inexperience, parents regard the first child as more difficult in a number of ways, even though objective ratings of temperament show that firstborn infants are no different from subsequent ones. There is no biological reason why a firstborn child should be more prone to extreme fussiness, and as for psychological reasons—well, this is just a variation of the maternal anxiety argument. Many studies have clearly shown that extreme fussiness occurs as commonly among subsequent infants as among firstborns.

There may be what we call a reporting bias at work here. A mother may simply deny—or refuse to believe herself— that a second, third, or fourth child has extreme fussiness. If her first child did not have extreme fussiness, she is perplexed: "It's not supposed to happen this way; I wonder what went wrong." If her first child did have extreme fussiness, she has even stronger emotional reasons for denying that it has happened again. Perhaps she still feels a little guilty about causing it in her first born. Perhaps she didn't get satisfaction from her doctor and doesn't see any point in bringing it up this time. Perhaps she feels that two extremely fussy babies are a certain sign of her doing something terribly wrong. This is bad luck, nothing more. Careful examination of mothers' reports of crying and fussy behavior in subsequent-born children shows that they are often identical to most definitions of extreme fussiness.

Then again, some mothers just face it. I had a mother tell me, with a tone in her voice as though she were being punished, "I survived not sleeping for three months with the first two; I guess I can do it again. Anyway, those children are fine now so we'll just wait it out." Try to tell this mother that extreme fussiness occurs only in firstborn children!

### Fallacy #8: Fresh Air Causes Extreme Fussiness.

Several mothers, primarily from rural backgrounds, have told me about "wind colic." The idea here is that taking a baby out in the night air or on a windy day causes cramps and great fussiness the next day. Some of these mothers even warn against leaving the window in a baby's room open at night. There is a long tradition of believing that "night air" causes all sorts of illnesses, but it is no truer in the case of extreme fussiness than anything else.

### Fallacy #9: Boys Get It More Than Girls.

The only explanation for this fallacy is that mothers might perceive problems in their sons more often than in their daughters, boys being thought more mischievous, active, and stubborn than girls. At any rate, it is not true. A study by the Canadian pediatrician, Dr. W.C. Taylor, and other studies agree that infant boys and girls share an equal risk in developing extreme fussiness.

*Fallacy #10: Better-Educated Mothers Have More
Extremely Fussy Babies.*

It sounds fanciful, but many people believe that the higher the mother's education level and social class, the more prone to extreme fussiness her baby is. You will also hear it stated in the contrary way: Extreme fussiness is less common among families of lower social class status.

These fallacies probably come from the patient selection bias of most pediatric training programs. Pediatric residents often learn from, and practice their skills on, poorer families who do not have private pediatricians. These families tend to visit emergency rooms and clinics sporadically, and often delay seeking medical care. Complaints of extreme fussiness may be less frequent among these families when compared to middle-class families leisurely discussing infant behavior in their private pediatrician's office. Then again, perhaps better-educated mothers read too many child-care books. Perhaps they are too quick to decide that normal crying is extreme fussiness. Perhaps they are less tolerant of whining and crying.

Careful studies show that social class or maternal education level bears no relationship to extreme fussiness. As part of my own studies, I have examined detailed, narrative descriptions of infant behavior and fussy periods. There is no question in my mind that extreme fussiness behavior, whether the parents call it extreme fussiness or something else, occurs equally among all social classes.

*Fallacy #11: Extremely Fussy Babies Are More
Intelligent.*

You may hear it said that children with extreme fussiness are more intelligent than others, or grow up to be more ambitious, driven, persistent, or ambitious. No study has ever supported or refuted this fallacy. Pediatricians generally recognize it as a "white lie" intended to help the parents live through this difficult period.

Here we have eleven common myths about extreme fussiness laid, I hope, to rest. Believing in or acting on any of these ideas cannot necessarily help you. It can distract, upset and exhaust you. Better to learn what we know for certain about extreme fussiness, and use this knowledge to act constructively on behalf of your infant, family, and self.

### Why So Many Myths?

Why is there so much misinformation about extreme fussiness around? Partly, as I have said, because of a lack of real factual information—mythology loves a vacuum. Also, the definition of extreme fussiness has been so vague that people have included only those cases that fit their pet theories and excluded those that don't. Most responsible, I believe, is our human tendency to see cause-and-effect relationships in what are only coincidences. This tendency is particularly frequent in the case of extreme fussiness, which varies inexplicably from day to day.

Consider these examples: A mother might take her baby out in the cool air one night and the next day he might have an especially bad extreme fussiness spell; she decides that the night air caused the extreme fussiness. A breastfeeding mother might stop eating gas producing vegetables; the baby may then have a couple of relatively quiet days; she decides that vegetables caused the extreme fussiness. Perhaps one baby's extreme fussiness has run its course at the same time his mother switched to a new formula; she may tell all her friends that Formula X causes extreme fussiness. A person may know three boy babies with extreme fussiness and no girl babies; he may conclude that boys have more extreme fussiness than girls do.

These are all errors. But you can see how the old wives' tales in this chapter got started, and how they seemed to be "proved" just often enough to keep them alive. While some of the "causes" may seem to explain a small number of cases, and while the "cures" may seem to work for a couple of days, in the long run none of them holds up.

# 4

## What We Actually Know About Extreme Fussiness

What researchers tell us about extreme fussiness is nowhere near as colorful as what magazines and mothers-in-law tell us, but the former is a lot closer to the truth. I believe that the unromantic facts about extreme fussiness must be better publicized if parents are to face extreme fussiness calmly.

This is not to say that every study by a person with letters after his or her name deserves our attention. Many of the extreme fussiness myths cited in the last chapter have been started or confirmed by reputable doctors doing, what appeared at the time, to be serious research. In every case, however, we can go back and see that there were flaws in the way the research was conducted. Perhaps the sample size was too small, the definition of extreme fussiness too vague, the evaluation too subjective. For example, some of these studies depended on parents' recollections of past behavior; these retrospective studies are considered quite unreliable. In other cases, researchers did not protect against their expectations coloring their findings, or failed to use statistical analysis to make sure that the connections they observed could not have occurred by chance alone.

Fortunately, medical research is constantly reevaluated. A new generation of doctors conducts new kinds of experi-

ments, and if these do not back up current beliefs, those beliefs have to change. In this way, older extreme fussiness research—research which "proves" that diet, inherited allergy,
or a neurotic mother is to blame—has by now been pretty
well discredited. Unfortunately, the news has not gotten
around as well as it should have.

In this chapter I will summarize what I consider to be
the key findings of several of the best-conducted extreme
fussiness studies during the past forty years. Not every point
in every one of these papers is equally valid, in my opinion.
I have cited here only those findings which have stood the
test of time and which I believe are correct. On the whole,
each of these studies has contributed importantly to ex-
ploding myths and adding to our knowledge of the facts.
These are the milestones in our current understanding of
what extreme fussiness is—or, I should say, what extreme
fussiness is not.

### What Kind Of Research?

You may be surprised that so little work has been
done on the causes of extreme fussiness. Most people think
that research always involves looking inside the body, trying
to understand what chain of physiological events—what hormones, chemical changes, electrical impulses, glands, nerves,
or organs—can lead to a certain condition. Physiological research into something as elusive and self-limiting as extreme
fussiness is almost prohibitively difficult. For instance, most
of the usual research tools are inappropriate. An important
and sometimes overlooked fact is that no animals appear to
suffer from anything like extreme fussiness.

No child ever died of extreme fussiness, so autopsies are
happily out of the question. Extreme fussiness is not serious
enough to justify anything more intrusive than an occasional
blood sample or x-ray. Yet, nothing about extreme fussiness
has ever showed up in blood samples or x-rays—not to men-
tion the fact that the patients are only a month or two old,

that they are not hospitalized and that the parents do not want to cause them any additional distress.

So you can see that until more subtle experimental procedures are developed and more frequent experiments conducted, we cannot learn about the actual organic mechanisms of extreme fussiness. And until we understand at least some of the physiology behind extreme fussiness, we will probably not be able to understand it very well. There is some irony in the condition of extreme fussiness; if it were a graver condition, we would know more about it.

With what I might call "internal work" on extreme fussiness so difficult, most studies approach it from the outside instead. That is to say, researchers observe a large number of babies with extreme fussiness and try to see what they have in common. This allows for generalization about incidence and the usual course of extreme fussiness. The researchers can explore links between extreme fussiness and other physical, environmental or temperamental variables. They compare extremely fussy babies with non-fussy babies to see if there are any significant differences between the groups that might explain why one group cries a lot and the other doesn't. This kind of research work asks questions like does extreme fussiness often appear to correlate with a history of allergy in the family? Do boys seem to get extreme fussiness more often than girls do? Do babies with extreme fussiness have, on average, more frequent bowel movements than babies without extreme fussiness? Questions like these can be answered without doing anything more to the baby than making his mother answer a lot of questions, and as we saw in the last chapter, if the study is not well designed, only serve to generate more fallacies.

Research like this will not give us the answers tomorrow but it is very valuable. First, it can define the usual course of extreme fussiness, to reassure parents that their baby is neither unusual nor ill. Second, it can help us deal with extreme fussiness even before we understand it. Knowing that it is a futile exercise to have the mother keep changing her diet, for example, is certainly worthwhile.

All of the studies below fall into the category of quantitative research. Most began as attempts to prove or disprove some commonly held beliefs about extreme fussiness. As you will see, the common beliefs almost always ended up being disproved. However, everything we can rule out as not being related to extreme fussiness brings us closer to understanding what is related to extreme fussiness, and what we can do about it.

### Dr. Illingworth: It's Not Allergy, Gas or Spoiling

Our understanding of extreme fussiness study dates from 1954, when Dr. R.S. Illingworth published his paper " 'Three Months' Colic." Dr. Illingworth, an English pediatrician who wrote several popular and influential books on childcare, is a British equivalent to our late Dr. Spock. Dr. Illingworth's landmark paper includes an exhaustive, and frequently humorous, review of the medical literature on extreme fussiness up until that time. He summarizes the assertions of some forty papers in many languages, detailing their contradictory and far-fetched theories on the causes and treatment of extreme fussiness. He found that the most persistent theories involved underfeeding, overfeeding, allergy, flatulence and spoiling, among others.

In order to get a base of factual information to prove or disprove these theories, Dr. Illingworth performed a careful study of his own. At the Jessop Hospital for Women in Sheffield, England, he studied fifty extremely fussy babies under three months old whose behavior could best be summed up by the following definition: " . . . said by their mothers to have violent, rhythmical screaming attacks, which did not stop when they were picked up, and for which no cause, such as underfeeding, could be found."

About 20 percent of the babies the doctor saw in the clinic behaved this way. Every time he found a baby with extreme fussiness, he enlisted the next baby to come in to the clinic, provided that baby had no excessive crying, as part of a control group. In this way, he had two randomly chosen groups of fifty babies each, more or less identical except for the extreme fussiness, which he could compare.

Dr. Illingworth saw all one hundred babies personally and followed up on them for six months. He collected a great deal of data about them, and their families. Most information, by necessity, came from reports by the mothers and not from his direct observation.

Dr. Illingworth was able to report these data: forty-four of the fifty had developed extreme fussiness during the first two weeks of life. In all fifty, extreme fussiness spells always occurred in the evening; in eight, the spells also occurred at other times but became much worse in the evening. Typically, extreme fussiness symptoms began between 6:00 P.M. and 9:00 P.M. and lasted from one to six hours. (This reminds me of one father who called his extremely fussy little son Dr. Jekyll and Mr. Hyde: when the sun went down the monster came out!) In many of the babies, feeding eased the symptoms for a brief time. Extreme fussiness disappeared, on the average, at nine and a half weeks. In twelve weeks 85 percent of the babies were over it; by four months all of them were over it. Comparing the extreme fussiness group to the non-fussy group, Dr. Illingworth concluded that extreme fussiness did not appear related in any way to the factors that had been suggested:

Underfeeding? The fifty extremely fussy babies gained more weight, on average, than the fifty non-fussy babies did. Some of the non-fussy babies who gained weight poorly did no unusual crying, while many of the extremely fussy babies had very good gains.

Overfeeding? "I firmly believe that for practical purposes, overfeeding in a young baby is a myth. It is so rare that one can truthfully say that it practically never occurs," Illingworth wrote.

Allergy? There was as much family history of allergy among the babies in the control group as among the extreme fussiness group. Only seven of the fifty extreme fussiness mothers said that their eating certain foods had any bearing on the child's extreme fussiness, and all named different foods!

Stomach or intestinal problems? To address this crucial old question, Dr. Illingworth x-rayed seven of the extremely fussy babies at the heights of their spells to see if there was excessive gas in their intestines. None showed up. To make sure there was no bias, Dr. Illingworth had these x-rays mixed in with a number of x-rays of non-fussy babies and challenged a disinterested radiologist to pick out the seven that were different. The radiologist could not pick out a single one. Barium enemas were also performed during the extreme fussiness spells. No malformation, obstruction, or spasms in the intestines were found.

A previous study in 1952 by Dr. S. Jorup at the Samaritan Children's Hospital in Stockholm also used x-ray studies obtained during the extreme fussiness spells. He also found no increased intestinal gas connected to extreme fussiness. As further evidence that digestive problems are not to blame, Dr. Illingworth found that the incidence of vomiting and the frequency of stools were the same for both extreme fussiness and non-fussy groups.

As for spoiling as a cause of extreme fussiness crying, Dr. Illingworth had this to say: "It is difficult to understand why rhythmical attacks of screaming, which do not stop when the baby is picked up and such as only occur with pain, should be ascribed to over-permissiveness' on the part of the mother. . . . Any parent who has possessed a child with extreme fussiness knows that it is the most worrying and disturbing complaint, and that a baby with obvious pain has to be picked up and cuddled."

In addition, factors which might bear on spoiling, such as the age of the mother and whether the baby is her firstborn and whether other children in the family had extreme fussiness, appeared identical for both the extreme fussiness group and the control group. In addition to deflating these five key claims about extreme fussiness, Dr. Illingworth was able to rule out these other factors:

*Table 2*

## FACTORS RELATING TO INFANTS
## THAT DO NOT INFLUENCE
## EXTREME FUSSINESS

Age of the mother
Parity of the mother (how many children she has had before)
Maternal illness during pregnancy
Number of fetal hiccups
Family history of allergy
Allergy in infant during the first six months
Sex of baby
Birth weight of baby
Weight gain of infant
Number of feedings per day
Method of feeding (breast versus formula)
Amount of spitting or vomiting
Number of stools per day
Increased muscle tone

In other words, the group of babies with extreme fussiness showed no more allergy, no difference in the frequency of feedings, didn't have younger or older mothers, etc. than the group of babies without extreme fussiness.

### Dr. Wessel: It's Not Allergy and It's Not The Family

Also in 1954, Dr. Morris A. Wessel and four associates at the Yale University School of Medicine published results of another extensive extreme fussiness project. They had begun work with a strong suspicion that allergy was responsible for a great deal of what they called "paroxysmal fussing" (extreme fussiness), and wanted to test this and other hypotheses.

Over the course of several years, a great deal of data had been collected on approximately two hundred mother-infant pairs who had passed through Yale's maternity and early infancy project. Data included prenatal interviews, detailed records of the infant's first week, follow-up reports by pediatricians, plus reports from a social worker and psychologist.

Dr. Wessel and his associates sent a questionnaire about family history of allergy to every mother who had been involved; ninety-eight of the women filled out and returned the questionnaire, which formed the basis for the Wessel study.

Fifty of the ninety-eight infants were judged to be "contented," and forty-eight to be "fussy." Of the forty-eight fussy infants, twenty-five were rated "seriously fussy," or "colicky," according to the following definition: " . . . one who, otherwise healthy and well-fed, has paroxysms of irritability, fussing or crying lasting for a total of more than three hours a day, and occurring on more than three days in any one week . . . Their paroxysms continued to recur for more than three weeks or became so severe that the pediatrician felt that medication was indicated."

Irritability, fussing, **or** crying for more than 3 hours total a day, for more than 3 days a week, and continuing for more than 3 weeks has become a standard definition of colic or extreme fussiness. The word '**or**' in the definition is important because many of these babies cry very little or not at all due to the heroic efforts of their mothers and fathers to soothe them. If these parents were to suspend their soothing efforts, then their baby would cry. The truth is that endless hours of soothing will often prevent crying. Wessel himself focused on 'fussiness' not 'crying' as the major problem when he titled his paper "Paroxysmal fussing in infancy, sometimes called 'colic' ".

Please note that there is a built-in problem with this definition: It expands the definition of extreme fussiness to include the pediatrician's behavior as well as the infant's! Whether or not the doctor feels medication is needed probably has less to do with the baby's condition than with the doctor's own training, tolerance, experiences with extreme fussiness, and how much pressure he is getting from the parents.

The ninety-eight mothers kept detailed diaries of their children's crying patterns, eating habits, bowel movements, weight gain, and general behavior. Thus, Dr. Wessel and associates were able to make many comparisons among the contented babies, the fussy babies and the extremely fussy babies.

The theory about allergy quickly proved invalid. There was as much family history of allergy among the contented infants as among the extremely fussy ones. Likewise, there were no significant differences in type of feeding, weight gain, sex, birth order, family history of extreme fussiness, and mother's education level.

Dr. Wessel's study confirmed many of Dr. Illingworth's findings as listed in Table 2, and adds several more:

*Table 3*

## FACTORS THAT DO NOT RELATE TO EXTREME FUSSINESS

Educational status of mother
Family history of extreme fussiness
Family tension

### Dr. Paradise: It's Not the Mother's Personality

Directly confronting the question of whether a mother's emotional state contributes to extreme fussiness, Dr. Jack L. Paradise published an extremely useful study in 1966. It was a prospective study, meaning that information was gathered as the babies developed rather than relying on the parents' recollections, and it used a standardized scale to rate the mother's personality, rather than relying on an interviewer's subjective impressions.

Dr. Paradise had been an assistant at the Rochester (Minn.) Child Health Services. He studied 153 full-term infants who were born at a certain hospital during a certain five-month period. This provided a good random sample because he took every baby and did not have a selection bias. A few of the mothers declined to participate and a few babies got sick and had to be dropped from the study so he ended up reporting on 146 infants out of the initial 153. He interviewed each mother at least once a month for three months. He gathered information about the baby's crying, eating, bowel habits, and the mother's own attitude. He examined the babies frequently.

Twenty-three percent of the infants turned out to have extreme fussiness, defined as:

> "Unexplained episodes of sustained crying of moderate severity occurring often enough to be considered troublesome or distressing; holding or rocking resulted only in partial or inconsistent relief" or "prolonged and intense periods of crying or screaming throughout the first three months or longer, not lessened by any attempted method of control, and of overriding concern to the mother".

As you see, Dr. Paradise has brought the reaction of the mother into the equation along with the infant's behavior. He has also used terms such as "sustained crying," "moderate severity," and "intense crying" without explanation or further definition. Any observer of infant behavior knows how hard it is to determine whether crying is "moderate" or "severe." And of course what causes "overriding concern" to one mother may not greatly disturb another. Despite these limitations, Dr. Paradise's study is important because of the way he evaluated the mothers' personalities. He had each of the 146 women complete the Minnesota Multiphasic Personality Inventory (MMPI), a widely accepted measure of personality characteristics. The MMPI includes 500 questions and a number of scales designed to correct for distortions that might be caused by illiteracy, defensiveness, or lying. It is a subtle and proven test which has been used on so many people that there is a large database with which the mothers could be compared. With MMPI results (computer-scored) in hand, Dr. Paradise looked for signs of those emotional disorders which previous studies had found connected with extreme fussiness: overall psychological disorder, anxiety, "rejection of the female or maternal role," and lack of energy or enthusiasm. For each of these, he took the mothers who scored the highest (for example, the most anxious) and those who scored lowest (least anxious), and found that extreme fussiness was equally common among the children of both groups. He was thus able to eliminate all of these personality disorders as connected in any way with extreme fussiness:

> The occurrence of extreme fussiness showed no relationship to maternal emotional factors, whether estimated clinically or measured by a standardized psychological test. Most mothers of infants with extreme fussiness were stable, cheerful, and feminine. He concludes that his evidence " . . . does not support the frequently stated view that colic (extreme fussiness) results from an unfavorable emotional climate created by an inexperienced, anxious, hostile, or unmotherly mother. By so advising parents, physicians may relieve them of unwarranted self-blame and anxiety."

Dr. Paradise's study also covered some of the same ground as Illingworth and Wessel, confirming their findings. To the list of factors unrelated to extreme fussiness, he added:

*Table 4*

## FACTORS THAT DO NOT RELATE TO EXTREME FUSSINESS

Amount of constipation, diarrhea, or flatulence
Type of formula
Duration of each feeding
Father's occupation
Maternal intelligence
Family history of gastrointestinal problems
Birth order of infant

## Dr. Stewart: It's Tension

A behaviorally oriented textbook has recently revived the notion that unexplained fussiness results from tension, caused by external overstimulation. The paper even uses the term "stimulus-overload extreme fussiness." The author argues, based only on his observations, that a child who cannot be consoled is signaling that he needs to be left alone to discharge tension by "crying it out." The author claims that letting an inconsolably fussy baby cry him to sleep several times will end, or permanently reduce, the crying. I find this hard to believe. Three months' extreme fussiness is not a behavioral problem. It cannot be prevented or cured. It is never a good idea to leave a very young infant to cry for hours at a time.

The not-so-hidden message here is that parental attempts to comfort an extremely fussy baby can be counterproductive. Suddenly we are back to the idea that parents can cause or at least aggravate extreme fussiness, either by overstimulating the baby physically or by passing their tension to him. Proponents of this theory like to talk about a vicious cycle of mounting tension between baby and parents. Dr. Brazelton speculated that overreacting parents can drive hypersensitive babies to greater and greater agitation, so that "what starts out as a two-hour period of crying rapidly grows to four, eight and twelve hours." An earlier study by Dr. A.H. Stewart similarly proposes that extreme fussiness occurs when unusually sensitive children are matched with unusually stimulating or unusually anxious parents.

The study conducted by Dr. Stewart in 1953 is at the source of the "tension" debate. This paper is so full of muddled reasoning and near slander against mothers and fathers of extremely fussy babies that I am surprised to see its message still taken seriously. This shows what mischief a few unfounded conclusions can cause.

Stewart studied a small group of infant-parent pairs to see if "excessively fussy" babies received different treatment than did "quiet" babies. They did. The mothers of the fussy babies reportedly jiggled, rocked and carried their babies more; changed the babies' positions more frequently; talked to them more loudly and for longer periods. Stewart—offering no evidence beyond her own observations—implied that all this activity caused the fussiness, as if the babies were being pestered and jiggled to the point of breakdown. Does this follow? I don't think so. If it is possible that a lot of handling can cause the fussiness, it is equally possible that the fussiness can lead to a lot of handling. Every mother tries first one thing and then another when her baby cries. Mothers of babies who cry a great deal develop a whole repertoire of consoling motions and sounds. These responses might not appear effective to a researcher during a brief observation, but over the long run this patting and bouncing and talking could well help. Concluding that a mother's comforting gestures are the cause of her baby's distress appears unfounded.

Stewart made a similar error in claiming that inconsistent parenting also caused the fussiness. She reported that the mothers of the seriously fussy babies in her study alternated between holding for long stretches and not holding at all, between overfeeding and underfeeding, between over-attentiveness and neglect. I doubt that any but the most distraught mothers behave as negligently and erratically as Stewart makes it appear, but I do believe that mothers of extremely fussy infants do behave inconsistently toward their babies. This is to be expected; extreme fussiness changes from day to day; what seemed to comfort the baby this morning might not work tonight. A mother who tries to remain consistent in her response to a wildly fluctuating condition will be left behind. An extremely fussy baby needs a flexible, adaptive, improvisational kind of management. The inconsistent behavior which Stewart suspects of inflaming, if not causing, extreme fussiness is more likely a reaction to it, and an appropriate one at that.

What of the theory that an infant can "pick up" tension from his parents? This is one of those oft-repeated ideas, which has no basis in fact. Brazelton says that tension in the people around a crying infant makes the infant's intestinal tract act up, causing the pain, gas, drawn-up knees, and behave extremely fussy, as though extreme fussiness were some sort of infantile ulcer! Stewart says that when a tense, anxious, or ambivalent parent holds the baby, the tension is communicated through all the baby's senses (including smell!). This is folk medicine at best. At worst, it is another twist on blaming the mother's behavior, personality, or her perfectly natural anxiety.

I continue to believe that attempting to console your extremely fussy baby through whatever means occur to you is the best approach. Something inside your baby is causing his distress. Your soothing motions, murmuring sounds, and close holding can only help. Of course, it is important that you do not let yourself become exhausted, depressed, or tense. The calmer you are, the more help you will be to your baby, and the better you and the rest of your family will come through this brief but trying period of extreme fussiness.

### Dr. Schnall and Dr. Shaver: It's Not Maternal Anxiety

Two subsequent studies have used objective psychological ratings to analyze whether there is a connection between a mother's emotional state and her child's extreme fussiness.

Dr. R. Schnall and his associates examined thirteen extremely fussy infants who were brought to the Royal Children's Hospital Clinic in Parkville, Australia. They asked the children's mothers to complete a standardized test called the Eysenk Personality Inventory. As a control group, thirteen non-fussy infants and their mothers were selected, and the same test was used. Dr. Schnall found no more neurosis or anxiety among the mothers of the extreme fussiness children than among the mothers of the non-fussy children.

Dr. Benjamin Shaver prefaced his report by reviewing earlier studies that had claimed that extreme fussiness stemmed from a baby's perception of her mother's anxiety. Dr. Shaver wrote:

"We agree with these authors that babies are exceptionally sensitive to their mother's mood. However, extreme fussiness rarely begins before the second or third week of life. If extreme fussiness were due primarily to the mother's mood and level of anxiety, we would expect the symptoms to begin in the first few days of life when the mother is the most anxious and unsure of herself . . . Also, we would expect the first-born of several children to be the most extreme fussiness prone. This is not the case, however, for the ordinal position within the family does not appear to be correlated with development of extreme fussiness."

With these points in mind, Shaver analyzed a sample of fifty-seven mothers, from the second trimester of pregnancy through the six postpartum months. The babies of twelve of these mothers turned out to have extreme fussiness (defined by Shaver as "excessive night crying").

To evaluate the mothers' moods, anxiety levels, and adaptation to motherhood, Dr. Shaver chose several characteristics to measure. These included "amount of physical contact," "sensitivity to infant's cues," "sense of humor," and "sense of success as a wife." On all of these items he compared the twelve extreme fussiness mothers to the other forty-five. On none of these measures did the mothers of the extremely fussy infants show any differences from the other mothers in terms of personality, or in success at adapting to motherhood. However, Dr. Shaver did find that extreme fussiness could temporarily disturb the mother-child relationship. The mothers of the extremely fussy babies were less confident and less accepting of their infants when interviewed around the child's three-month birthdays. This should not surprise anyone who has experienced or can imagine three months of screaming and crying. When Dr. Shaver repeated these measurements at six months—after the extreme fussiness had passed—the mothers of the formerly extremely fussy babies were indistinguishable from the control group: they had gotten their confidence back and accepted their babies most readily. Apparently mothers are as remarkably resilient as their suffering babies.

### Urinary Tract Infection?

The suspicion that extreme fussiness might be caused by an unrecognized urinary tract infection has generated a lot of speculation. Physicians and parents have spent time waiting to collect urine specimens; infants have endured painful bladder punctures and catheterizations, and infants have been given unnecessary antibiotics. The study, which led to this unfortunate state of affairs, is called "Colic as the Sole Symptom of Urinary Tract Infection in Infants," This is a misleading title.

In this study, again, no real definition of extreme fussiness was used; only "the appearance of paroxysmal abdominal pain." Only four infants were reported, all of who were so sick as to require hospitalization (definitions of extreme fussiness usually state that infants are thriving and gaining weight normally). Moreover, two of the four babies were six months old at the time of the diagnosis of extreme fussiness. Extreme fussiness does not occur at the age of six months. Therefore, the concept of urinary tract infections as a cause of extreme fussiness should be critically restudied. Naturally, infants at any age with poor weight gain, fever and chronic irritability should be evaluated for any disease, including urinary tract infections.

### Drugs During Labor?

A paper "Drugs During Labor May Disturb Normal Behavioral Development," by an Australian physician named Dr. David Thomas, focused on epidural anesthesia during labor as a cause of extreme fussiness. Epidural anesthesia does appear to affect both infant behavior and maternal perceptions for a short period after delivery. However,

Thomas went much further. He suggested that drugs administered to the laboring mother pass through the placenta so that the baby is born with high drug levels in his blood. The drug levels fall after delivery and, of course, no drug is administered to the infant. So what causes the extreme fussiness in the infant, Thomas speculates, is in fact drug withdrawal. No specific definition of extreme fussiness was used. In fact, Thomas acknowledged that the assessment of extreme fussiness is difficult because it can depend on the subjective feelings of the mother and the researcher. Also, the investigator who decided which babies had extreme fussiness knew ahead of time which mothers had received epidural anesthesia. Preconceived biases might have influenced his diagnoses. The findings in this study would be more convincing if the assessment of which infant had extreme fussiness had been done in a blind fashion.

### Gastroesophageal Reflux

Babies do 'wet burps,' spit ups, and vomit during infancy. It appears to be effortless; she can smile at you and puke on you at the same time! All babies naturally do this and parents have to learn to protect their clothing and furniture. It is unwanted and undesirable, but it is not a medical problem in the vast majority of babies. To reduce or prevent this behavior, pediatricians, may use drugs. However, there is no data linking gastroesophageal reflux to fussiness or crying in infants. Nevertheless, some children are medicated under the fanciful notion that the baby is suffering from pain like the 'heartburn' of indigestion.

### Naturally Occurring Substances May Cause Extreme Fussiness

**Prostaglandins** are powerful muscle contractors. For example, it is probably prostaglandins that cause contraction of the uterus, and thus the cramps of dysmenorrhea.

They might also cause spasm of the smooth muscle in the lung, leading to breathing difficulties. Prostaglandins can similarly contract the muscles lining the intestine.

These chemicals are therapeutically administered to certain infants with birth defects involving the heart. In one study, the authors observed irritability in two infants who had received therapeutic prostaglandins for heart disease. If their observation is confirmed on a larger number of infants, we might be able to conclude those high levels of prostaglandins—occurring naturally or administered therapeutically—might cause extreme fussiness. New research on prostaglandins and similar chemicals has focused on the unregulated overproduction or the unbalanced production of these substances. We do not yet understand how the tight metabolic control processes work when we are healthy. However, the observations that fatty acids influence the production of these chemicals should lead to exciting research regarding the nutritional composition of breast milk and baby formulas.

**Progesterone** is a hormone made by the placenta. Generally, the infant is exposed to very high levels of progesterone at birth. A provocative old study suggests that progesterone deficiency might be a cause of extreme fussiness. The authors of that study observed that uterine smooth muscle contractions during labor are accompanied by a fall in the mother's progesterone level. Those authors wondered if extreme fussiness might in fact come from similar painful smooth muscle contractions (perhaps of the smooth muscle in the intestine) caused by low progesterone levels. Perhaps extremely fussy infants make an abnormally low amount of progesterone. High levels of progesterone from the placenta would protect these infants during the first few days of life, explaining why extreme fussiness has a delayed onset after birth.

Progesterone deficiency as a cause of extreme fussiness is an attractive hypothesis because progesterone, and its related chemical products, are potent central nervous system depressors. For example, in adults large doses can induce sleep

or anesthesia. It would make sense that infants wi
progesterone levels—and thus less central nervous syst
depression—might be more intense, fretful, difficult to
soothe, easily startled, and have more difficulty staying
asleep for long stretches.

Unfortunately, the authors of the first progesterone study
also did not use an explicit definition of extreme fussiness.
Further, they did not "blindly" evaluate their claim that a
progesterone-like drug successfully treated extreme fussiness.
Additionally, they used a crude urinary analysis technique to
determine progesterone deficiency.

To improve upon this study, we at the Children's Memorial Hospital measured plasma progesterone levels in twenty-
five infants at a few weeks of age, when progesterone from
their mothers would no longer be present. Infants were divided into two groups: those with extreme fussiness (according to Wessel's criteria), difficult temperaments or low
sensory threshold; and those without any of these features.
One researcher measured plasma progesterone levels while a
different researcher, working independently, made the diagnosis of extreme fussiness or no extreme fussiness. We found
that among the infants with extreme fussiness, difficult temperament, or low sensory threshold, plasma progesterone
levels were unusually low. These infants also slept for shorter
periods of time and awoke more frequently at night. However, in a larger study that compared only infants with and
without extreme fussiness, regardless of subsequent temperament diagnosis, the group differences in levels of progesterone were less impressive, although extremely fussy
babies still had lower levels.

**Melatonin** is a hormone produced by the pineal gland lo-
cated deep within the brain. The mother's pineal gland produces melatonin that crosses the placenta. The concentration
of melatonin is high around the time of delivery and remains
high only for several days after the baby is born. Then, the
levels become extremely low in the baby until three to four
months of age at which time the baby begins to produce her
own melatonin. Also, at three to four months of age, the se-

ns to show a light/day pattern in which
uring the day and higher levels occur at
at this hormone is capable of causing
it is sensitive to light-dark cycles, and it
n of the smooth muscle of the intestine.
d by my wife and myself suggests the following role for melatonin in producing extreme fussiness:

During the first several days of life, high maternally derived melatonin causes the baby to be very sleepy, drowsy,
and calm. During the next few months, the absence of this
inhibiting hormone allows the baby to wake up and to become more alert. The baby becomes more wakeful. The gut
is bathed in naturally occurring chemicals which have high
levels in the evening or night, such as serotonin, which cause
contractions of the gut. The imbalance between serotonin
and melatonin during the first three to four months causes
cramping abdominal pain and the absence of melatonin also
causes extreme wakefulness that is painful.

### "Exterogestation"

The word "exterogestation" means that during the
first few months of life, because babies behave in many ways
like a fetus, the baby is still continuing the gestation period
even though it is outside the womb. It's as if human babies
are born too soon! At first glance this seems to be a strange
idea, so please be patient while I explain it to you. First, the
rapid growth of babies during the first several months after
they are born is similar to the rapid growth of all other primates before they are born. Second, in other primates, the
brain growth rate slows soon after birth, but in our babies,
the brain grows rapidly after birth. Third, when you compare
gestational durations, onset of puberty, and total life spans
for all other primates, the data suggest that human babies
have too short a gestational period. How come? The answer
is simple. In order to walk in an upright fashion, the bones
of the pelvis and hip region changed and made the birth
canal smaller. As humans developed larger brains, it became

necessary for human babies to be born earlier and more 'immature' compared with other primates.

This may explain why it takes 3-4 months for some systems such as the ability to produce melatonin in response to light/dark cues, the ability to have regular day and night sleep periods, and other systems to mature. This is also the age after which Sudden Infant Death Syndrome no longer occurs. This is also the age when extreme fussiness subsides and ends.

A consequence of this relative immaturity might be that during the first few months, babies are more comfortable, feeling as if they were in the womb, when they are swaddled and being rocked. Swaddling and rhythmic rocking movements are two of the three main methods used to calm babies. The third is to encourage sucking. Swaddling is relatively ineffective in older infants perhaps because they no longer need to feel like they are in the womb. Some researchers believe that this immaturity of human infants at birth creates such severe helplessness of the newborn that the mother is compelled to be extremely attentive to the needs of her baby, and that this nurturing attention evolves into maternal attachment or love for her baby.

Another observation derived from animal studies is that ducklings pipe, lambs bleat, and monkeys make distress vocalizations **only** when they are away from their mother. These 'cries' have been described as 'proximity promoting behaviors' because they draw the mother to her baby for feeding, protection, and comfort. Similarly, when our babies cry, it is a signal drawing parents toward their baby. It's as if the cry unleashes parental attachment and love.

Extreme fussiness/colic seems to not occur in any other animal. Maybe this is because human babies are born 'too soon' and the fuss/cry signal, which is part of the baby-mother attachment system, is imperfectly recognizing the world outside the womb. It's as if to say that the baby, being born 'too early' is actually **unaware** that the mother is, in fact, present. Thus, the baby fusses or cries even when the mother is present and soothing her baby.

As with all biologic measurements, there would be a range of immaturity causing a range of fussiness/crying so that some babies had more and some babies had less. Additionally, the ability for the baby to even start to make a fuss/cry signal requires about 40 weeks gestation so that babies born prematurely do not have more fuss/cry behavior compared to babies born at full term.

### *Several Physiological Disturbances*

Extreme fussiness may be the outward expression of more than one disturbance. There are not that many ways that a one- or two-month-old bundle of organs and nerve endings can express discomfort and/or some kind of physical disharmony—long periods of crying is one, inability to sleep well is another. It is probably wrong to think that every baby diagnosed as "extreme fussiness" suffers the same underlying problems. I suspect that the reason one cause of extreme fussiness has eluded us for so long is that there isn't just one.

There are probably several related or unrelated physiological disturbances that are capable of causing extreme fussiness. In some instances, the predominant symptom might be the fussing spells; in other instances the fussing might be less of a problem than the symptom of inability to sleep well. The problems may not be entirely physiological; and it is also possible that different physiological disturbances in infants of no real medical significance trigger irregular, inconsistent or deliberately inattentive parenting, which in turn aggravates (not causes) excessive crying, sleep disturbances, and/or difficult temperaments.

### *The State of the Art of Extreme Fussiness*

As you can see, we know much more about what extreme fussiness is not, than what it is. It is a poorly understood complaint and quite distressing. Studying extreme fussiness is complicated, and in fact most research has been done around the edges of extreme fussiness rather than at its core cause.

All studies agree on some things. Extreme fussiness occurs in about 20 percent of all babies. These babies may experience periods of explosive, inconsolable crying with the appearance of abdominal pain and gassiness. The outbursts of unmanageable and disagreeable behavior usually start during the first two weeks, occur mainly in the evening, and typically disappear by three to five months of age. The cause of extreme fussiness is unknown, but factors such as birth order, sex, parental social class, allergy, maternal intelligence, maternal anxiety, and maternal personality have not proven to be involved.

It seems to me that any researcher who seriously maintains that the mother causes extreme fussiness will have to explain three interesting facts. First, why does extreme fussiness nearly always begin within two to three weeks of birth in full-terms babies, and within two to three weeks of expected birth dates in premature babies? Even if you maintain that the child has to be with the mother (outside of the womb) a few weeks to feel the full burden of her anxiety, why would a premature baby not fuss until she has been living with her mother six, seven, or eight weeks? Second, why isn't extreme fussiness confined to, or at least much more common among firstborn babies? Mothers are demonstrably more anxious around their first infant, but all studies agree that extreme fussiness occurs as often among second born children as among firstborn. Third, why is extreme fussiness almost universally worse in the late afternoon and evening? A mother's anxiety follows no daily pattern; why should a child's response follow one? Some doctors have suggested that a mother is more fatigued as the day goes on, or becomes anxious over the father's return home from work. Frankly, mothers of extremely fussy infants are fatigued and anxious all the time. Even when an infant's "day" runs from one in the afternoon to midnight, even when the mother works outside the home and does not see the baby until evening, even when the father works the night shift, extreme fussiness stubbornly worsens at 6:00 P.M. or 7:00 P.M. no matter what.

I believe that these three facts point to a physiological rather than an environmental cause for extreme fussiness. I believe that a maternal anxiety explanation simply leaves too many questions unanswered. I want parents to know that tension in the family is simply not the answer to what causes extreme fussiness.

Review all of the factors listed in Tables 2, 3, and 4. These are things we can say with confidence do not have any direct connection with extreme fussiness. So if you fear that your own anxiety, or your husband's allergies, or your smoking or breast milk or level of education, or your fondness for lima beans is causing your child's misery—reassure yourself. We do not understand the causes of extreme fussiness, but I am absolutely assured that it is not the parents' fault.

# 5

## How Is Extreme Fussiness Related to Ordinary Fussiness/Crying?

Some of the things we know about crying in general shed some light on extreme fussiness. This information is helpful to parents who are distressed by their child's crying, even though they might not be facing a full-fledged case of extreme fussiness.

Parents often ask me why their babies cry at such inconvenient hours! In truth, these nighttime crybabies also cry during the day when such crying is less bothersome and makes less of an impression. Become sensitive to the fact that there are gradations between the best and worst of crying time. It might be worthwhile to keep a detailed diary so that you can separate the observations from your perceptions. Even babies who cry a lot have good times too!

It is hard to be objective about crying. Crying is an irritating sound. It seems to bespeak misery and pain. It is impossible to ignore. There is something about it that "poisons the atmosphere," as one mother put it. You can't sleep, enjoy a meal, or concentrate on something else while you can hear your baby crying. This is considered a survival mechanism that must have developed during our evolution. It must be nature's way of making sure your baby gets attention when he needs it.

*What Does Crying Mean?*

Since crying is one of the few ways a newborn infant can communicate, it is open to interpretation. We may think that a crying baby is hurting, or frightened or angry, or it can be taken as criticism, loneliness or tension.

Tennyson wrote in "In Memoriam":

> But what am I?
> An infant crying in the night;
> An infant crying for the light;
> And with no language but a cry.

There's something in all of us that identifies with a crying baby. Who hasn't felt alone in a strange world, cold, confused, and unable to communicate? We project onto a sobbing child all the despair of our human condition. But I think it is important to realize that we really don't know what a baby's crying means. Although babies do cry when they have been hurt or had a fright, it is not right to assume that a baby is hurting or scared whenever he cries. We don't even know for sure that a crying baby is unhappy. Perhaps the folk wisdom is right that says babies cry, "to exercise their lungs," or simply because it's one of the few things they know how to do. Birds fly, babies cry.

Above all, remember that a screaming infant is not "doing a number" on you. Infants do not cry to manipulate, punish, or annoy you. They do not know yet that their crying can get results. They do not even know that they are a separate person from you. They are just crying. Perhaps they know why they are crying even less than you do.

*What Should Parents Do About Crying?*

Illingworth noted that one cause of crying is fatigue. This might suggest that you should leave a tired baby alone to cry him to sleep. But Illingworth categorically states that

during the first few weeks of life an infant should be consoled rather than left alone. He claimed that picking up a
baby when he or she cries will result in less crying later on.
This has been verified by the direct observational study by
Silvia Bell and Mary Ainsworth at Johns Hopkins University
in 1972. They disproved the notion that always responding to
a newborn's cry will encourage crying behavior.

### You Can't Spoil Your Newborn

Bell and Ainsworth focused on twenty-six white,
middle-class, infant-mother pairs. Data was gathered by observing these mothers and children at home. The observers
confirmed first of all that all infants have some crying spells.
They noted the number of crying episodes that a mother ignored, the number she responded to, the length of time it
took her to respond, what kind of response she made, how
effective it was, and the overall effectiveness of the mother in
making the baby stop crying. Picking up a baby and holding
him proved to be the most effective way of terminating crying. Talking to him or gesturing at him from a distance was
the least effective.

Bell and Ainsworth observed that some mothers were deliberately unresponsive when the baby cried, for fear they
might spoil the baby. However, data from the study showed
the contrary: mothers who consistently and promptly responded to their infants' crying were rewarded with infants
who at the age of one year cried less frequently, and for
shorter durations, than those infants whose mothers ignored
crying, or who delayed a long time in responding.

The authors of that study concluded that infant crying is
so disagreeable or "change worthy" to adults that it probably
serves a useful biological function. They think that infant
crying should be viewed as an "attachment behavior" or
"proximity promoting" behavior because it serves to bring
the mother closer to the child. Mothers cannot ignore their
baby's crying. The Bell and Ainsworth study showed that a
mother should not struggle to overcome the natural impulse

to comfort her crying child. An infant less than three months of age, it appears, is at no risk of being spoiled.

This bears out many studies of infants that suggest that conditioning or training a very young baby is very difficult, even in a carefully controlled laboratory environment. Spoiling, after all, is simply teaching undesirable behavior. Babies under a few months of age maybe cannot "learn" a crying habit because they are not neurologically mature enough. Remember that a baby is not neurologically mature enough at three weeks of age to learn to smile specifically at her mother. Specific social smiling at parents naturally develops at about six weeks (in prematures, this occurs at about six weeks after the expected date of delivery). If you cannot teach a baby to smile before she is neurologically ready, why assume you can teach her to cry?

However, studies performed after the Bell and Ainsworth study strongly suggest that you can teach a crying habit to children over six months of age by indiscriminately responding to all vocalizations and always picking them up and soothing them. These children then appear to learn to cry more for more attention. In contrast, for children over six months of age, parents who discriminately respond to cries that appear to be intense or related to hunger or soiling and do not respond to quiet whimpers, mild calls, low level whining sounds have children at one year of age who, in general, cry less.

### Frequent and Infrequent Criers

Bell and Ainsworth also observed that the frequency of crying showed "individual stability" between nine and twelve months of age. Babies under nine months of age did not show much of a pattern regarding frequency or duration of crying spells, but after nine months a baby could be identified as a frequent or infrequent crier, and this identification proved to hold true as the child grew older. We can infer that infrequent criers were those babies whose mothers had always responded promptly in the early months and perhaps became more discriminately responsive after several months.

Other studies confirmed that the frequency of spontaneous crying spells is a relatively stable individual characteristic after nine months of age.

### Similarities between Extreme Fussiness/Colic and Ordinary Fussiness/Crying

Several studies of normal crying show that the line between ordinary fussiness/crying and what we call "extreme fussiness/colic" is often indistinct. In five fundamental ways, ordinary fussiness/crying mimics the patterns associated with extreme fussiness/colic.

### 1. All Babies Cry Some of the Time

Crying in infants was first intensively studied in 1945 by a group of dedicated researchers at the Mayo Clinic. In their first study, they observed seventy-two babies in a newborn nursery. They worked in shifts so that each baby was observed twenty-four hours a day. The observers recorded the onset of crying and how long it lasted. They tried to attribute a cause to the crying—wet or soiled diapers, hunger, cramped positions, chilling and the like—if one was apparent. They found that most of the newborns cried between one and eleven minutes per hour. The average daily total duration of crying was about **two hours** for these seventy-two babies.

Continuous observations were made while the babies were in the nursery for eight days—the recommended stay at that time. Remember that these babies were being observed every minute during those eight days. Researchers found that the minimum amount of crying per day was 48 minute; the maximum amount was 243 minutes. All of the infants cried some of the time—at least 48 minutes per day. As mentioned above, and it bears restatement, the average duration of crying was about two hours per day.

## 2. Some Crying Can't Be Attributed to an Obvious Cause

The researchers attempted to classify the causes of crying: hunger, vomiting, wet or soiled diapers, and unknown reasons. For example, if the baby was crying and sucking around feeding times, and was calmed by feeding, then the crying was attributed to hunger. They found that hunger appeared to cause 36 percent of all time spent crying. A wet diaper caused about 21 percent of crying time and soiled diapers about 8 percent. Specifically interesting was that 35 percent of all crying was due to "unknown reasons." The researchers were surprised that such a large part of crying—over one-third—could not be explained by any obvious causes.

Then they examined the number of separate crying spells. Each spell was counted once, regardless of its duration. They found that the number of spells for "unknown reasons" were greater than any other cause, including hunger. Their conclusion: crying spells caused by hunger were slightly longer in duration, though less frequent, than those caused by "unknown reasons."

This is an important point. Babies have more crying spells for "unknown reasons" then they do for known reasons such as being hungry, wet, or soiled. Also, the number of individual crying spells per day for American, Dutch, and !Kung San African babies is the same. What is different, however, is that the !Kung San babies are never hungry because they are breast fed about four times per hour so that they have shorter duration of crying spells. The !Kung San babies are always held and the mother responds to the weakest fret within seconds. By having shorter duration spells, but the same number of spells, the !Kung San babies have less crying.

This suggests the possibility that parents by promptly and continuously attending to their baby's fussing might be able to prevent ordinary fussing/crying from escalating into ex-

treme fussiness/colic. I'll discuss this more later, but now let's
return to that Mayo study.

The findings of the Mayo study, then, were that all babies
cry during the newborn period and that much of this crying
cannot be attributed to any obvious cause. The authors made
some guesses about non-obvious causes: bright lights, peri-
staltic movements or contractions in the gut, loud noises,
loss of equilibrium. They added, almost as an afterthought,
that perhaps the infants' crying expressed a need for fondling
or rhythmic motion.

The authors continued the study on a smaller group of
forty-two infants from the original sample, using a detailed
diary filled in by the mothers at home. This data covered
about twenty-one days at home, after a nine- or ten-day stay
in the nursery. The babies averaged four crying spells a day.
**All** babies had some crying spells. Fifty-five percent of these
spells were attributed to hunger. Crying for 'unknown reasons" occurred in 20% of babies. Again, "unknown reasons"
seemed to be second only to hunger as a cause of crying.
Crying associated with vomiting, stooling, urination, over-
heating, bathing, chilling, lights or noises (the mothers making these attributions) were individually less common than
crying "for unknown reasons."

### 3. Two to Three Hours' Crying Per Day is Average.

The well-known Cambridge pediatrician T. Berry Brazelton performed an important study on crying in 1962. He
used diaries completed by parents to study crying in eight infants. Fussiness/ crying spells unrelated to hunger or to wet
or soiled diapers occurred in virtually all the babies. Only
twelve of the eighty fussed less than one and one half-hours
per day. About half cried for about **two hours** per day. This
increased to an average of about **three hours** per day at age
six weeks. Thereafter the amount of crying declined to about
one hour per day by age twelve weeks.

**4. Many Babies Have Evening Crying Spells.**

Brazelton also found that crying spells became much more focused or concentrated in the evening by the time the infants were about six weeks of age. By this time, very little crying occurred during the day. The spells of crying in the evening proved to be predictable and began suddenly. The reason for this rapid shift in behavior from a calm/quiet state to a crying state is not known.

**5. Crying Decreases at About Three Months.**

Brazelton found that, on average, crying decreased to about one hour per day by age twelve weeks. Another Harvard study verified Dr. Brazelton's observations using tape recordings of infants crying in their homes. They observed the same time course: an increase in crying at about six weeks and a decrease by about twelve weeks. This means that the natural history of unexplained crying runs the same time course as that of extreme fussiness behavior. In both cases, babies calmed down at about three months of age. Also at this time a stable individual pattern of crying behavior that will hold true for at least the next year seems to develop. This general pattern of increasing fussiness/crying peaking about six weeks of age and then decreasing occurs in all babies, in all cultures, including the !Kung San.

*Extreme Fussiness/Colic May Just Be a Lot of Ordinary Fussiness/Crying*

You can see that, in at least five important particulars, what we have been calling "extreme fussiness/colic" is just an extreme form of ordinary fussiness/crying. Brazelton suggested that those infants in his study who cried more than the others were indistinguishable from infants with extreme fussiness/colic. I think this is a very plausible suggestion. There is not a great gulf between normal crying and extreme fussiness. The idea that extreme fussiness is an all-or-nothing event (like pregnancy) is probably wrong. Extremely fussy babies may sometimes cry like other babies, only more so. Or, if you prefer, normal babies cry like extremely fussy babies, only less so. The greatest difference between normal crying and extreme fussiness—amount and day-to-day variation—shows up clearly when crying behavior is put into graph form. Below are charts of three general patterns of infant crying. There are gradations among them, of course, and no baby fits any one pattern perfectly.

Figure 1 shows the most common pattern of "normal" infant crying, including "unexplained fussiness." It should reassure mothers who, noticing that their infant's crying has increased to around three hours a day by six weeks, worry that this increase in crying will continue and turn into extreme fussiness. This usually never happens. Also, many nursing mothers report "feeding problems" around six weeks. This is because sucking is soothing and mothers often confuse fussiness with hunger. Your baby will suck whether your baby is hungry or fussy, but your baby doesn't suck with a strong force or interest when fussy. Remember that six weeks

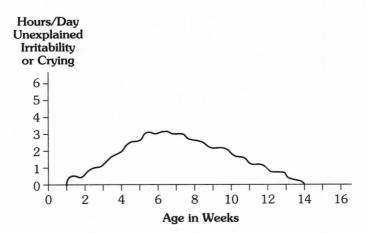

**Figure 1.** Unexplained fussiness; spares first few days; about two hours/day at two weeks of age; three hours/day at six weeks of age; and one hour/day at twelve weeks of age.

is usually the normal peak of unexplained fussiness and has nothing to do with hunger or dehydration. 'Treatments' given around six weeks of age appear to 'work' because the baby was about ready to naturally calm down anyway.

Figure 2 shows in a general way what extreme fussiness/colic looks like. As you can see, the onset of prolonged crying occurs shortly after birth.

Figure 3 describes infants who, for a few weeks, appear to be developing extreme fussiness but never actually do. After a few days or several days (not three weeks) of excessive fussing/cry they settle down into a pattern resembling Figure 1. Doctors who treat these babies during their fussy first weeks might claim that they have cured extreme fussiness, but the reduction in crying is spontaneous. It is never appropriate to make a diagnosis of extreme fussiness until after more than three weeks of age.

When mothers are allowed to describe their infant's behavior in their own words, several traits become apparent. The descriptions of the extreme fussiness period are remarkably consistent. It is impossible to detect differences based on the sex of the child, the social class or age of the mother, or the birth order.

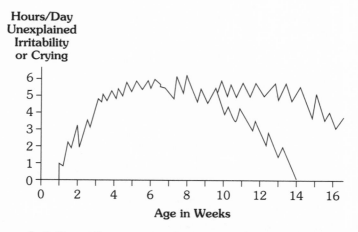

**Figure 2.** Colic rapidly increases to three or more hours a day with great variation day to day, and might last longer than three months.

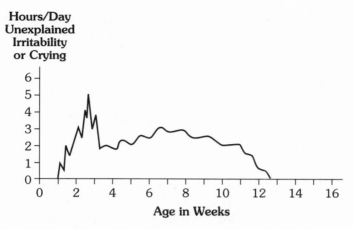

**Figure 3.** Burst of unexplained fussiness resembling colic, but lasting only a few weeks or only a few days.

In addition, detailed interviews with hundreds of mothers whose infants had extreme fussiness, and a study of diaries they kept of their infant's behavior, makes it clear to me that the salient feature of extreme fussiness crying is its erratic pattern from day to day.

Sometimes the extreme fussiness crying is rhythmical; sometimes it is a persistent monotone. The crying infant may be easily consoled on one day and absolutely impossible to console the next day. Sometimes infants are consolable in the morning and inconsolable that very same night. Days may occur without any extreme fussiness spells, and the duration of spells may vary considerably from day to day or within a given day. Nearly all mothers describe rapid and unexplained changes in mood. This seems to be a characteristic of extreme fussiness. I cannot believe that changes this abrupt would occur unless there were one or several physiological triggering mechanisms.

The message of this chapter has been that extreme fussiness is an unusual amount of normal fussiness. Some researchers and parents object. They say that extreme fussiness crying is different from other kinds of crying in quality. Extreme fussiness/colic, they say, sounds different. I agree that a baby in an extremely fussy spell sounds different from a baby who has received a shot, for instance. I know that mothers can make even finer distinctions. My wife says that for our four children, the hunger cry was persistent, the tired cry was whining and less forceful, and the extreme fussiness cry was harsh. Tape recordings reveal that the paroxysmal crying of extremely fussy babies is remarkably similar from one baby to another.

As best I can describe it, extreme fussiness crying is droning, monotonous, almost mechanical-sounding. It does not have the highs and lows, silences, gasps, moans and sobs of pain crying, or hunger crying. In fact, if we weren't predisposed to call every loud, repetitive, annoying vocalization made by a baby "crying," the noise of extreme fussiness might have a name of its own. To me, some extreme fussiness crying is closer to wheezing or gasping than to crying.

We are back to the idea that extreme fussiness is an abnormally large amount of normal fussiness and crying. The question remains, why do some babies get so wound up in their fussiness that they go on for three, six, twelve hours at a stretch, while most babies fuss/cry for only a couple of hours a day?

### Which Babies Cry More?

Brazelton suggested that the more "fussy" infants in his study—the ones whom we might call extreme fussiness—had a distinct type of personality. They seemed to him more active or sensitive.

Illingworth came to a similar conclusion much earlier. In a 1955 paper called "Crying in Infants and Children," he wrote that the amount of crying for an individual baby is related to the personality of the baby, and that placid and easy babies cry less than determined and difficult babies. He speculated that during the first three months of life, crying is due to loneliness or a desire to be picked up. Perhaps some babies feel this need more acutely, or express it more persistently, than others.

Possibly the difference is physical: something which causes all babies a little distress bothers extremely fussy babies much more. Possibly it is a question of sensitivity: extremely fussy babies are continually disturbed by stimuli which other babies can ignore. Possibly it is a question of temperament: not all babies are able to calm themselves down at the same rate, and extremely fussy babies may be unable to calm themselves down at all. It does seem that babies with extreme fussiness tend to be more determined, sensitive, and difficult to manage.

You will read more about the temperament connection in the next chapter. In the meantime, remember that your extreme fussiness infant is not doing anything that other babies don't do. She is just doing it a little more persistently.

# 6

# Infant Temperament
# and Extreme fussiness

Some parents can be philosophical about extreme fussiness. They can say, "Well, he's just that kind of baby." They may be right. There turns out to be a significant association between extreme fussiness and a certain kind of infant personality. One mother asked me if we could cure her fussy baby by performing a personality transplant!

That newborn babies have personalities is not news. Every mother of twins or triplets knows that this is true. Your baby has an individual style of behavior at a very early age. Some mothers know before delivery that their baby will be unusually active. When babies are only thirty hours old, temperament differences between ethnic groups can be measured. Behavioral differences present at birth might reflect inherited or genetic traits. They might also be acquired traits, possibly reflecting environmental influences during pregnancy. Many child development specialists believe that both genetic and environmental factors combine to affect the behavior of newborn infants.

*Extreme Fussiness Personality?*

Table 1 described extremely fussy infants as vigorous, intense, energetic. As you read in the last chapter Dr. Brazelton has called extremely fussy infants active and sensitive. Dr. Jorup in his classic study mentions that extremely fussy babies are excessively sensitive to sound and light, sleep for unusually short periods, and seem restless in general.

What is the truth about extreme fussiness and a certain kind of temperament? Since temperament is such a subjective factor, could an extreme fussiness temperament even be measured?

*A Standardized Temperament Rating*

All parents naturally make their own assessments of their babies' temperaments. You may be surprised to know that there is a standardized system for evaluating infant temperament. It is not absolutely objective, and it has a number of limitations that I will point out later, but it has proved over the years to be very useful and statistically sound.

The researchers who developed this system, Drs. W.B. Carey and S.C. McDevitt, did not have extreme fussiness anywhere in their minds. There is not even a crying dimension in their system. No one correlated temperament, as rated on this scale, with extreme fussiness until much later. However, as you will see, the correlation proved to be striking.

*Infant Temperament Characteristics*

Carey and McDevitt refined their method of measuring infant temperament in 1977. Starting with nine characteristics that had been described earlier by Alexander Thomas and Stella Chess of New York University, Carey and McDevitt developed a parent-response questionnaire

that has been widely used around the world. It measures the
following temperament traits:

## 1. Activity.

Does the infant squirm, bounce, or kick while lying awake
in a crib? Does she move around when asleep? Does she
kick or grab during diapering? Some infants always appear
to be active, others only in specific circumstances, such as
bathing. Activity levels in infants have nothing to do with
"hyperactivity" in older children. I have examined a few babies who previously had been referred to a pediatric gas-
troenterologist because of extreme fussiness. When he
recognized that there were no gastrointestinal problems, he
decided that the problem was "hyperactivity." This diagnosis was made on the false notion that wakeful, reactive, or
difficult infants are hyperactive. There is no proven association between extreme fussiness in infancy and hyperactivity
when older.

## 2. Rhythmicity.

Rhythmicity is a measure of how regular or predictable
the infant appears. Is there a pattern in the time he is hungry,
how much he eats at each feeding, how often bowel movements occur, when he gets sleepy, when he awakens, when he
appears most active and when he gets fussy? As infants grow
older, they tend to become more regular in their habits. Still,
some babies are very predictable at age two months, while
other babies seem to be irregular throughout the first year.

## 3. Approach/Withdrawal.

Approach/withdrawal is a temperament characteristic
defining the infant's initial reaction to something new. What
does he do when meeting another child or a baby sitter? Does
he object to new procedures? Some infants reach out in new

circumstances; accept, appear curious, approach; others object, reject, turn away, appear shy or withdraw.

## 4. Adaptability.

Adaptability is measured by observing such activities as whether the infant accepts nail cutting without protest, accepts bathing without resistance, accepts changes in feeding schedule, accepts strangers within fifteen minutes and accepts new foods.

## 5. Intensity.

Intensity is the degree of an infant's response, either pleasant or unpleasant. Think of it as the amount of energy with which they express their likes and dislikes. So intense infants react loudly with much expression of likes or dislikes. During feeding they are vigorous in accepting or resisting food. They react strongly to abrupt exposure to bright lights; they greet a new toy with enthusiastic positive or negative expressions; they display much feeling during bathing, diapering or dressing; and they react strongly to strangers or familiar people. One mother described her extremely fussy baby's intense all-or-nothing reactions: "Her mood changes quickly; she gives no warning—she can go from loud and happy to screaming." Intensity is measured separately from mood.

## 6. Mood.

If intensity is the degree of response, mood is the direction. It is measured in the same situations described above. Negative mood is the presence of fussy crying behavior or the absence of smiles, laughs, or coos. Positive mood is the absence of fussy crying behavior or the presence of smiles, laughs, or coos. Most intense infants also tend to be more negative in mood than positive.

## 7. Persistence.

Persistence level, or attention span, is a measure of how long the infant engages in activity. Parents may value this trait under some circumstances, but not under others. For instance, persistence is desirable when the child is trying to learn something new, like reaching for a rattle, but it is undesirable when the infant persists in throwing food on the floor. Unfortunately, some babies persist in their prolonged crying spells and their prolonged wakeful periods. One father described his persistently crying baby as follows: "We have a copper-top alkaline battery-powered baby and we're powered by regular carbon batteries. He outlasts us every time."

## 8. Distractibility.

Distractibility describes how easily the baby may be distracted by external events. Picking up the infant easily consoles a distractible infant's sleep or hunger; soothing can stop fussing during a diaper change. New toys or unusual noises easily distract the infant. Distractibility and persistence are not related to each other, and neither trait is related to activity or threshold levels.

## 9. Threshold.

Threshold levels measure how stimulus sensitive the infant is in specific circumstances, such as those previously discussed. While some infants are very reactive or responsive to external or environmental changes, other infants barely react.

To determine a temperament profile you would rate your baby on a six-point scale for each of the ninety-five questions about his behavior. For example:

| | Almost Never | Rarely | Variable Usually Does Not | Variable Usually Does | Frequently | Almost Always |
|---|---|---|---|---|---|---|
| The infant reacts strongly to foods whether positively (smacks lips, laughs, squeaks), or negatively (cries) | 1 | 2 | 3 | 4 | 5 | 6 |
| The infant cries when left to play alone. | 1 | 2 | 3 | 4 | 5 | 6 |

(The first question is about the *intensity* and the second question is about *mood*.)

### *"Difficult Temperament"*

While observing many children and analyzing many questionnaires, Dr. A. Thomas and Dr. S. Chess noticed that some of these temperamental traits tended to cluster together. For example, infants who were extreme or "intense" in their reactions also tended to be slowly adaptable, negative in mood, and withdrawn. This appeared to be a personality type.

According to their parents' descriptions and direct observation by the researchers, these infants seemed more difficult to manage than other infants. Consequently, a child whose scores fall into this pattern is said to have a "difficult" temperament. Some mothers refer to these infants as "mother killers." Infants with the opposite temperamental traits are said to have "easy" temperaments. These are sometimes called "dream" babies. One father described his "easy" infant as a "low maintenance baby."

Of the original group of infants Thomas and Chess studied, about 10 percent fell into the difficult temperament category. These infants also tended to be irregular in biologic function such as sleep schedules and night awakenings. They were more likely to have behavioral problems—particularly sleep disturbances—when they grew older. One of the most interesting differences between difficult and easy babies is the way they cry when they are past the extreme fussiness period. Recently published research found that mothers listening to the taped cries of infants rated difficult (not their own babies), described the crying as more irritable, grating, arousing than the crying of easy infants. They said that the first group sounded spoiled and were crying out of frustration rather than hunger or wet diapers. An audio analysis of the cries helped explain why this should be. The crying of the difficult infants was found to have more silent pauses between crying noises than that of the easy babies. Also, at its most intense, the crying of difficult infants was actually pitched at a higher frequency. These two differences can make the crying seem much more frightening, piercing, and annoying.

Why do babies with difficult temperaments cry this way? Do they learn to do it? Is it genetically prewired? Is it connected with other factors that make up a difficult temperament? These are questions that should be explored.

Some professionals contend that the diagnosis of difficult temperament paves the way for future behavioral problems, but in general using infant temperament ratings to predict future development is controversial at best. Many pediatricians have a natural disinclination to label or give undue emphasis to any behavior just because it is at one end or the other of an arbitrary continuum. They also do not like to attach labels that have negative implications. They point out that unusual behavior in adults is accepted as an "idiosyncrasy" or "eccentricity" and can in fact indicate intelligence, creativity, or a drive to achieve. Some claim that "undesirable" infant character traits mature into adult virtues. For example, the trait 'persistence' drives you crazy when you child persists doing something that you do not want him to do; but the same trait might be likned to 'ambition' later on which fosters achieving success. Certainly children with so-called difficult temperaments are every bit as lovable and promising as easy children. They are just a bit more of a handful for their parents. A difficult temperament diagnosis is useful only if it can help parents be prepared and understanding.

### Limitations of Temperament Measures

I want to make it clear what the Temperament Profile is, and is not. It is a statistical tool used to describe groups of babies. It is not a very good way to evaluate one specific baby; your own observations are much better. What the Profile does is to put into fairly simply, numerical terms that infinitely complex structure called personality. When done on large numbers of infants, it provides a reliable standard for studies that seek to relate certain factors (in our case, extreme fussiness) to temperament. But using the results obtained for one infant to make predictions about his or her future is an unsound business. If your child should be given one of these tests, and if you are told the results, remember that it is just a snapshot, and a blurred one at that.

There is a certain built-in limitation to the Profile; ratings can be the obtained during the first few months of life but your baby does not really show stable behavior patterns yet. This is demonstrated when different rating instruments, The Carey Infant Temperament Questionnaire, the Brazelton Neonatal Assessment Scale, The Bayley Scales of Infant Development, used on the same infant, do not yield internally consistent results. Temperament measures obtained later, at age four to eight months, are moderately stable and can predict temperament measures taken for the next three to seven years.

Interestingly, this development of stability in temperament rating follows a time course parallel to that of crying behavior. After the first few months of life, the amount of crying a baby does—like the temperament traits he shows—develops into enduring characteristics.

Make sure you understand the time frame. When we talk about temperament and extreme fussiness, we are talking about a baby with extreme fussiness (before three or four months of age) developing into a baby with a certain kind of difficult temperament (not measured until after four months of age). We are measuring two different things at two different times.

Another limitation to the Temperament Profile is that the infant does not fill out the questionnaire himself. So the ratings might reflect the preconceptions, and in fact the temperament, of the mother who does the rating. Here we see one of the many built-in quandaries of studying very young children. Unless ingenious tests are devised, an adult must interpret everything. Perhaps it is fitting that this Profile measures both infant behaviors and parental perceptions. After all, how mother views her infant is probably as important for the mother-child relationship as is how the infant is actually behaving. There is as much a chance of problems developing when a mother merely perceives her infant to be "difficult" as when he is in fact, objectively, a difficult child. A dramatic example of the difficult child's behavior and parental response spiraling out of control would be child abuse.

A third limitation is that this Profile, including our definition of extreme fussiness, uses arbitrary criteria in order to put labels on things. But infant behavior is a continuum. It has no natural cut-off points. There are some children who are almost but not quite difficult enough in their behavior to earn the label "difficult," just as there are children who cry almost but not quite enough to be diagnosed as "extreme fussiness" or "colic." In addition, if an infant does not rate a difficult temperament, the parents and pediatrician should not assume that all would be rosy.

In spite of these limitations, there is value in using statistical analyses and numerical ratings to identify difficult temperament, and to find relationships between temperament and other dimensions of child development.

### Difficult Temperament and Extreme Fussiness

It is important to note that an infant's temperament does not appear to be associated with the infant's sex, birth order, or social class. It does not seem to be related to the method of feeding (breast or formula) or to birth weight. Curiously, it might be related to ethnic group; one study shows that Chinese infants are more difficult than non-Chinese infants are.

Most significant for our purposes, Carey found that difficult temperament is associated with extreme fussiness. He studied a group of infants with extreme fussiness. Later, when they were old enough to be given the Temperament Profile, four were treated as difficult, four as almost difficult, four as almost easy, and only one as easy. There was, as Carey noted, "a significant concentration in the first two groups." The association between difficult temperament and extreme fussiness might have appeared stronger if Carey had included those difficult children who had almost-but-not-quite-enough crying behavior to be called "extreme fussiness." Please remember that infant behavior is a continuum, while definitions, by their nature, impose arbitrary cut-off points.

My research has shown that when infants with extreme fussiness learn how to sleep well, after about four months of age, they are not likely to develop a "difficult" temperament.

Carey's findings do suggest that extreme fussiness is a combination of excessive but still normal crying plus a perfectly normal temperament, with tendencies toward intense reactions, slow adaptability, negative mood, withdrawal, and irregularity. These many behavioral tendencies which make up difficult temperament, and the crying of extreme fussiness, may be two facets of the same problem. One may, in some sense, cause the other. They may both have a common cause. Or, as we will explore in the next chapter, there may be a third factor in the equation.

If your baby seems "difficult," whether or not she had extreme fussiness, hug her, love her, and look forward to the time when she is older. Many parents find that their sour babies really do turn sweet after three or four months. You'll read about some examples in later chapters. There is hope that soon you will all sleep through the night and enjoy your days together as well.

# 7

## Is Extreme Fussiness
## a Sleep Disorder?

*Dr. Weissbluth: The Sleep Connection*

At the Children's Memorial Hospital in Chicago, my colleagues and I did our own study of extreme fussiness. We looked at many of the factors in Tables 2, 3, and 4, but we concentrated on possible relationships between extreme fussiness and sleep patterns.

Five pediatricians cooperated in our study. They asked the parents of patients, aged four to eight months, to complete our written questionnaire about their children's sleep patterns. The questions covered the time the child usually fell asleep, when he woke up in the morning, how often he awoke at night, and whether or not the child had had extreme fussiness. We received 202 questionnaires and after excluding children with medical problems that might have affected their sleep patterns, we ended up with a sample of 141. Twenty percent of them had suffered from extreme fussiness (as defined by Wessel).

We found that the following can be added to the list of factors that do **not** relate to extreme fussiness:

*Table 5*

## FACTORS THAT DO NOT RELATE
## TO EXTREME FUSSINESS

Hour asleep and hour awake
Duration of night awakenings
Parents' attempt to maintain regular sleep schedules
Parents' willingness to allow infant to cry himself to sleep
Consistency and promptness of parents' reaction when infant
    awakened at night and cried
Maternal prenatal smoking or caffeine consumption

However, we did find one significant difference between the babies who had been extremely fussy and those who had not. Infants who had extreme fussiness when younger than four months, awoke at night far more frequently than the others when they were four months old. They also tended to have less total sleep (day sleep plus night sleep) and to require more time to fall asleep. Remember that this is well after the extreme fussiness symptoms had disappeared. You will read more about the relationship between extreme fussiness and sleeping problems in later chapters.

I have referred before to an apparent connection between extreme fussiness and sleeping problems for the baby (that extreme fussiness can cause sleeping problems for the parents goes without saying). Some researchers have claimed that difficulty falling asleep and frequent night awakenings are an integral part of extreme fussiness. It has been my experience that sleeping problems may not be apparent while the extreme fussiness lasts—some extremely fussy babies exhaust themselves crying all evening and sleep soundly through the night—but they often show up later.

Let's review what we know about sleep in general, infant sleep and the connection between extreme fussiness and infant sleep.

### Newborn Sleep Patterns

At about six weeks of age, or six weeks after the due date for babies born early, **night sleep organization** develops. What does this mean? Before six week, the longest single sleep period is not very long and its occurrence is randomly distributed around clock time. In other words, there are many short sleep periods that occur totally unpredictably. But at about six weeks of age, there will be a 4-6 hour sleep period occurring in the evening or at night. This is night sleep organization. The end of "day-night confusion."

During the day, at 12-16 weeks of age, a mid-morning nap will emerge first and an early afternoon nap emerges second. Note that **day sleep organization** develops after **night sleep organizaton**.

Over these first sixteen weeks, there are gradual changes in the infant's sleeping pattern. There is a small decrease in the total hours asleep, a doubling of the longest sleep period, and an increase in the amount of sleep occurring at night. By sixteen weeks, most infants are sleeping about thirteen to seventeen hours per day and the longest sleep period is about seven to ten hours. Mothers often start feeding solid food with the hope of getting the child to sleep, but the introduction of solid foods does not alter the development of these sleep patterns. In general, by three to four months of age, most children are sleeping for longer periods of time, and primarily at night. As children become older the total amount they sleep decreases.

Your infant sleeps as long as previous generations slept. The age-specific sleep durations have not changed over the past sixty years. A study at the Children's Memorial Hospital in 1981 found today's sleep durations consistent with those measured in 1911 and 1927. The social changes in the past sixty years, differences in family size, and how people spend their time, the introduction of central heating and air conditioning, or television, VCR, and computers have also not had a significant impact on how much children sleep. This would lead us to believe that sleep patterns reflect physiological, genetic behavior as opposed to learned, environmental behavior.

### Sleeping Positions

Sleeping position does not affect sleep patterns after the first few days of life. Some newborns appear to cry less, move less, and sleep better on their stomachs. However, after a few weeks of age, some babies do sleep better on their backs. In England and China it is customary to place infants on their backs because of the fear that they might bury their heads into the mattress and suffocate. In the United States it used to be customary to keep babies on their stomachs because of the fear that they might vomit and choke. These are not reasonable fears; preferred sleeping positions in different countries only reflect different customs. We still do not know why some babies sleep better in one position or another. However, we know that the risk of Sudden Infant Death is less when babies sleep on their back. Therefore, please sleep your baby on her back.

### Understanding Sleep

Studies done in "sleep labs" have helped us to understand some of the mysteries of the state we call sleep. We have learned that the sleep of young infants is different from the sleep of older children.

### Sleep States

Sleep is not one constant state. Brain activity during sleep is not static and unvarying, like a TV test pattern. On the contrary, sleep is an active, multileveled, frequently changing condition. There are qualitative differences in sleep patterns throughout the night.

Sleep researchers have identified two basic sleep patterns. The "active" sleep state is called Rapid Eye Movement or REM sleep, because during this state, the eyes move back and forth rapidly under closed lids. REM sleep is associated with irregular breathing and heart rhythms and with many fleeting body movements. Dreaming mostly occurs during REM sleep. The opposite state, called non-REM sleep, is associated with decreasing body movements and slow, regular breathing and heart rhythms. The active (REM) and quiet (non-REM) sleep states alternate in a usually predictable fashion throughout the night.

### Newborns Have a Unique Sleep Pattern

Researchers have measured the number of REM periods, the duration of each individual REM period, the total duration of all REM periods per twenty-four hours, and the percent of total sleep time spent in REM sleep in subjects of all ages. They have found these measurements are basically similar for older infants, children and adults. A noteworthy exception is that newborns under the age of three months show a different pattern. This means that during the first few months of life, REM sleep patterns may be undergoing organization.

One way newborns differ is that younger infants spend much more time in the REM sleep state than do older children and adults. Another difference is that an infant under three months of age enters a REM state immediately upon falling asleep, while after three months sleep always starts with a non-REM period. Why this is, and why it changes at that age is not known.

Also, the cycle of alternating between the sleep states is much shorter in the infant than in the older child or adult. That is to say, each state lasts a shorter amount of time and one follows the other more quickly. It takes about four months to establish the periodic organization of sleep states, which will last throughout a lifetime.

**Day Sleep vs. Night Sleep**

Recent research on infants has focused on differences between daytime and nighttime sleep.

Less REM sleep. During the first three or four months of life, the following rearrangement occurs: REM sleep diminishes significantly during the **day**, as the number of daytime REM periods decreases, though the length of each stays about the same. In other words, fewer bouts of REM sleep but no change in the duration of each bout.

More non-REM sleep. At the same time, non-REM sleep increases during the **night** as the duration of each non-REM period increases significantly, though the number stays the same. In other words, longer bouts of non-REM sleep but no change in the number of bouts.

This is an example of how sleep evolves in a complex fashion. Fewer REM periods occur during the day and longer non-REM periods at night. The conclusion that I will lead you to is that not all sleep periods are created equally and that we should think of sleep quality, not just sleep quantity.

So the changes during the day are not exactly like those occurring at night. Something in a baby's nervous system causes a decrease in the number of REM sleep periods during the day and an increase in the duration of non-REM sleep periods during the night (Table 6). This may reflect what people mean when they say a baby has to learn to tell day from night, or to "get its best sleep during the night." Clearly there is a lot of behind-the-scenes activity. For little babies each twenty-four-hour period is divided into REM sleep, non-REM sleep, wakefulness, and something called ambiguous sleep because it looks a little like both REM and non-REM sleep.

**Possibility #1: Extreme Fussiness Is Disorganized Sleep**

Not all babies get their sleep organized at the same rate. Let's consider some of the possibilities for a two-month-old

*Table 6*

## CHANGES IN SLEEP PATTERNS
## FROM 0-3 MONTHS

|  | DAY SLEEP (NAPS) 8:00 A.M.-8:00 P.M. | NIGHT SLEEP 8:00 P.M.-8:00 A.M. | TOTAL SLEEP |
|---|---|---|---|
| REM Sleep | Fewer REM periods (no change in duration) | No change in number or duration | Less REM sleep |
| Non-REM Sleep | No change in number or duration | Longer duration of non-REM periods (no change in numbers) | More non-REM sleep |

baby. Sleep organization may have developed normally, with increasing long phases of non-REM sleep mainly at night. Or sleep organization might be delayed or abnormal, in which case we might see too many REM periods, or REM periods which are too long, or REM periods occurring at the wrong time. Sleep patterns can be disorganized either in terms of the number, duration, or timing of the sleep states.

What this means is that a lot of shifting between different sleep states is going on even though we can't see it except when the eyes are fluttering during REM sleep. Many researchers think that REM sleep has a stimulating effect on the baby's developing brain and this "internal" stimulation represents a biological form of learning. This is similar to "external" stimulation from the environment that triggers the wiring of the brain to learn languages, abstract concepts, and arithmetic. For adults and older children, it is thought that REM sleep is especially important for emotional or psychological restoration, to walk up feeling less stressed or tense. While non-REM sleep seems especially important to physically restore fatigued muscles, to erase the muscular weakness from being active all day and to restore a sense of physical vigor or strength.

The bottom line is that not all sleep is created equally. As sleep patterns develop, it is important to think of quality of sleep, not just quantity.

We do not know what it is in the baby's brain that orchestrates harmonious sleep patterns, nor do we know the effects of abnormal sleep patterns. Perhaps extreme fussiness results from internally disorganized sleep patterns. Alternatively sleep patterns might be desynchronized with other vital functions such as breathing control.

### Sleep and Breathing Rhythms

Some infants may develop the ability to sleep for long periods of time before they acquire the ability to control their breathing during these prolonged sleep periods, or during specific sleep states. The rate of breathing is a relatively stable individual characteristic—some infants tend to be fast breathers and some tend to be slow breathers. However, the rate of breathing during sleep is related to the specific sleep state: people always breathe faster during active sleep states and slower during quiet sleep states. This relationship between sleep state and breathing rate develops during the first few months of life.

It is possible that some babies have to cope with more asynchrony than others do. These babies might not be able to breathe regularly enough to keep themselves asleep. They may sometimes have to fight for air. What better way for a baby to keep her lungs inflated and get plenty of oxygen into her bloodstream than through several hours of lusty screaming?

Charles Darwin, in his book Expression of the Emotions of Men and Animals, was the first to point out the important breath-control component in crying. He described in great detail how during crying the arrangement of the facial muscles, gasping sounds, lingering shudders, and the way the nose clogs and the eyes close, can all be traced to changes in respiration. Crying, we might conclude, is a strange, overwrought kind of breathing. Extreme fussiness paroxysms might be more like breathless gasping than adult grief—or pain-related crying. It is not too much of a leap to suggest that when breathing becomes disordered because of a lack of coordination with the sleep cycles, the infant might compensate with spells of agitated persistent crying that we are calling extreme fussiness.

I believe that the sleep-breathing-crying connection might hold an answer not only to the puzzle of extreme fussiness, but to the tragedy of Sudden Infant Death Syndrome. That, too, might be some sort of sleep-related breathing disorder. It is, I believe, significant that when babies are having extreme fussiness spells, they are almost never SIDS victims.

### *Sleep, Temperature and Endocrine Rhythms*

If a sleep cycle, which is not yet synchronized with breathing, could cause an infant distress and lead to extreme fussiness, a sleep cycle not synchronized with temperatures or hormone rhythms could have the same effect.

Body temperatures and the levels of certain hormones go through predictable, daily ups and downs. These rhythms develop during the first year of life. During the first few months especially, temperature and hormone variations are quite irregular, but we now know that serum cortisol concentrations in the blood begins to show a pattern very early leading to a distinct twenty-four-hour pattern at about six months of age. Melatonin is another hormone that develops a regular night time peak at about three to four months of age.

Also in newborns, human growth hormone is secreted throughout a twenty-four-hour period. By four months of age the pattern of secretion becomes organized into a circadian pattern. That is, during every twenty-four-hour period there are dramatic differences between the highest and lowest hormone levels, and these peaks and valleys occur at about the same clock hour every day. Once the pattern is established, the hormone is released at night after the beginning of sleep, and most of the hormone is released during the deeper, later stages of sleep. We do not understand the chemical machinery which links sleep rhythms to endocrine rhythms, but these rhythms might offer a key to understanding extreme fussiness, especially why extreme fussiness so often occurs in the late afternoon or evening hours.

Many people, including Dr. Brazelton, explain "evening" extreme fussiness by saying that the child senses the mother's increasing eagerness/anxiety as the time comes for the father to return home. I think this is an ingenious but unfounded suggestion. It's an example of how male pediatricians or psychiatrists used to put the blame of everything undesirable about children on the mother!

Much more plausible is that the occurrence of most spells in the evening is related or linked to distorted biological rhythms.

Is extreme fussiness infant jet lag syndrome? Biological rhythms that are out of synchrony with the normal cues of daylight and darkness cause us to feel slightly sick, and jet lag syndrome in adults is an example of this. With jet lag syndrome, we may feel awake, alert, and attentive but have difficulty in thinking, focusing, or concentrating. Sometimes we ache or feel worn down, but we still can have difficulty in falling asleep. Another example of not feeling well because biological rhythms are out of synch with daylight cues are the symptoms experienced by shift workers. Sleep loss from those jobs that require you to be up at night cause headaches and stomach pains. Extreme fussiness certainly appears to be a painful condition, especially pain in the abdomen. Mothers of extremely fussy children who are up at night know that pain felt by shift workers is real pain.

Severe fatigue alone is painful: you ache. The inability to sleep well may cause painful fatigue.

So here is one possible line of inquiry that would link sleep with extreme fussiness: asynchrony between sleep-wake rhythms as they develop or asynchrony between sleep and temperature/hormone rhythms, and breathing rhythms may individually or together cause distress in an infant. The more disorganized these rhythms are the more severe the extreme fussiness behavior. Then, at three months or so, when the transition to a normal, adult sleep-cycle pattern is complete, the extreme fussiness may disappear, but not necessarily the sleep disorder.

## Possibility #2: Extreme Fussiness Is an "Acted-Out" REM Period

Studies in adults suggest that during Rapid Eye Movement sleep, the brain is similar to being "awake." During this time, the electroencephalogram superficially resembles alert wakefulness and vivid dreaming occurs—while the body is "paralyzed." This is not paralysis due simply to relaxed muscles. Rather, a neurologically active inhibition of muscles turns on during REM sleep.

In a study done on cats during REM sleep, this muscle inhibition was experimentally blocked and the cats behaved as if they were awake. They appeared to be hunting or pouncing on mice while asleep! Perhaps if a similar block were performed on humans (it involves potential permanent brain damage and could never actually be tried), we would appear to act out our dreams. One case where we can observe something like this phenomenon in humans is the shaking and jerky movements seen in alcoholics with delirium tremens. This seems to result from an uncoupling between active (REM) sleep and the muscle paralysis that usually goes with it.

Is it possible that the increased motor activity during an extremely fussy spell—twisting, turning, stiffening, and clenching—represents a breakthrough in this muscle inhibition? That the baby might be, in a sense, in a state of REM sleep without having yet fully developed the characteristic accompanying muscle paralysis? Typically, a child ends an extremely fussy spell by suddenly "falling asleep." This could, in fact, be the onset of a quiet (non-REM) sleep state.

### Asleep or Awake?

On the surface, it seems absurd to claim that a screaming, writhing baby is more asleep than awake. But in very young babies, the line between sleep and wakefulness is not all that clear. Often the electroencephalogram cannot distinguish between sleep and wakefulness until at least ten weeks of age. To distinguish between REM and non-REM sleep, measurements of eye and chin muscle activity, or of breathing and heart rhythms, must be taken. It is hard to tell exactly what state an infant is in during an extremely fussy spell. Behaviorally, during an extremely fussy spell babies appear to be "out of touch," inconsolable, and unreachable. Perhaps they are not really conscious.

If this is correct, then the fact that some babies have crying spells during which they are 'inconsolable' might mean that they are in a strange sleep state and thus beyond our reach.

Perhaps extreme fussiness occurs during a Rapid Eye Movement sleep period, then the writhing and screaming might be the behavioral reflection of dramatic shifts in breathing and body temperature which we know occur during REM sleep—shifts we usually don't see acted out because the muscle paralysis keeps the body still.

Indirect evidence suggesting an association between extreme fussiness and Rapid Eye Movement sleep was published by Dr. Robert Emde at the University of Colorado Medical Center in 1970. In a well-documented series of detailed observations, Dr. Emde noted that infants may appear to be awake—sucking, fussing, crying or smiling—at a time when rapid eye movements are observed under closed eyelids. These "active" behaviors during Rapid Eye Movement sleep tend to disappear by age three months. Over and over again, it appears that the age three to four months is a crucial turning point. Although it is only speculation, I suspect that unexplained fussing or extreme fussiness behavior in some infants is linked with this crying/Rapid Eye Movement sleep state.

Another study showed that intensive eye movements during sleep, called **REM storms**, occurred more often in those infants who showed dramatic "neurobehavioral instability." That is, these infants showed greater behavioral irregularity, or shifts in behavioral states, from week to week than other infants.

Extreme fussiness disappears at about age three months. Sleep-state control matures at about age three months. Each spell of extreme fussiness almost always terminates with the infant falling asleep. I doubt that all this is coincidence.

With the passage of time, your baby's developing brain becomes better able to inhibit, suppress, turn off, or tune down the ever-present background restless, random fidgety behaviors—both when awake and asleep. Also, circadian rhythms develop and become synchronized with each other and day/night schedules. If these are neurologically related events, then both possibility #1 (Extreme Fussiness Is Disorganized Sleep) and #2 (Extreme Fussiness is an "Acted-Out" REM Period) may be partially correct. The infant with disorganized biological rhythms might have his greatest distress at about the same time every day, and the child who lacks the active inhibitory development appears "wired" or "turned on" during the day and always seems to sleep in an active fashion (REM storms?). Extremely fussy babies usually behave as if they suffered from not enough sleep (too wakeful, too fatigued, too cranky), and too much crying at night. Extreme fussiness appears to be much more of a neurological developmental condition than a gastrointestinal problem, or a parental problem.

### The Crying Temperament—Sleep Connection

We have talked about extreme fussiness and excessive crying, extreme fussiness and difficult temperament, extreme fussiness and disorganized sleep. I believe that the eventual solution to the extreme fussiness puzzle will draw all of these factors together. For now, I can only suggest where the connections might be made.

Table 7 summarizes a frequently seen relationship between a certain kind of awake behavior and a certain kind of sleep pattern.

Infant temperament assessments taken between four and eight months, utilizing the questionnaire developed by Carey, showed a clear relationship between difficult temperament

*Table 7*

# RELATIONSHIP BETWEEN AWAKE BEHAVIOR AND SLEEP PATTERNS

| *AWAKE BEHAVIOR* | *SLEEP PATTERNS* |
|---|---|
| Colic | Sleeplessness, "insomnia" |
| Low sensory threshold | Easily aroused from sleep |
| Easily Startled | Increased frequency of night awakenings |
| Difficult temperament | Increased frequency of sleep/wake |
| Increased creying | transition per twenty-four hours |
| Active, vigorous | |

and brief sleep durations. Infants with a difficult temperament slept significantly less than infants with an easy temperament. Briefer sleep durations were also observed among infants with extreme fussiness. It is possible that insufficient sleep causes difficult temperament. Or common factors such as parental behavior and neurologic immaturity could influence both sleep duration and infant temperament.

Several other studies suggest a relationship (as shown in Table 7) between (1) extreme fussiness or excessive crying, (2) low sensory threshold, and (3) difficulty in sleeping—either brief sleep durations or frequent night awakenings.

"Low sensory threshold" refers to infants who are easily startled or who respond dramatically to small changes in their environment. In the study that connected temperament and extreme fussiness, Carey concluded that extreme fussiness was unusually common among infants who turned out to have difficult temperament and/or low sensory threshold. Sensory threshold is a component of temperament; however, it is not part of the easy/difficult diagnosis. Yet it does prove to have a parallel link to extreme fussiness. Carey also found that low sensory threshold was associated with frequent night awakenings.

My impression is that babies with extreme fussiness who learn to sleep well after three to four months of age do not develop a low sensory threshold. However, babies who had been extremely fussy during the first few months who subsequently do not learn to sleep well become more stimulus sensitive, easily startled, and easily upset . . . because they are severely over-tired!

A study at the Children's Memorial Hospital tied extreme fussiness to a definite increase in the frequency of night awakenings. Older studies have suggested that night waking in children (with or without extreme fussiness) is associated with brief sleep durations. Night waking also appears to be a problem associated with an abnormal sleep schedule.

Other studies at the Children's Memorial Hospital have showed that babies who are active, intense, and stimulus-sensitive, as determined by the Temperament Questionnaire, have more regular breathing when asleep at night, with fewer respiratory pauses than infants who are inactive, mild, and less responsive to environmental stimulation.

We have a set of convincing linkages here. Clearly, the problems of extreme fussiness: difficult temperament, low sensory threshold, frequent night awakenings, and brief sleep durations are interrelated. Perhaps these are different facets of the same problem. None of them tends to be subject to much parental influence in young infants. None shows much individual stability during the first months of an infant's life. All develop a sharper focus and more enduring pattern after about three months of age. This parallel time course, often occurring in one infant, suggests either that (1) time is required for infants to "learn" behavioral styles and sleep patterns, or (2) some physiological maturing takes place, or (3) both learning and maturing occur.

Support for a physiological view comes from several studies that show that extreme fussiness occurs in premature infants within a few weeks of the expected birth date, regardless of the gestational age at birth. In other words, extreme fussiness appears time-locked to biologic development counting from conception, not from birth. Extreme fussiness most likely has more to do with the physical, rather than the behavioral, maturing of the child.

*Extreme Fussiness May Be Part of a Larger Problem*

The evidence seems convincing that infants who suffer from extreme fussiness in their first few months of life have a better-than-average chance of difficult temperaments, and/or having sleeping problems later in their infancies. Researchers who feel strongly that extreme fussiness has no aftermath blame this connection on parents. They say that living with a screaming baby for three months causes parents permanently to change their behavior toward the child. They might, for example, become inattentive or "emotionally unavailable" to the child, either out of exhaustion and distress, or as a deliberate management tactic to prevent indulging their baby. It is this parental behavior which, according to this theory, causes behavior problems in the child.

My colleagues and I had a chance to test this theory when we conducted a study of the drug dicyclomine as a treatment for extreme fussiness. Several previous studies had indicated that dicyclomine can relieve the symptoms of extreme fussiness. We studied forty-eight extremely fussy infants, some given dicyclomine and some a placebo (plain cherry syrup), and found that dicyclomine is in many cases an effective treatment for extreme fussiness.

We figured that if dicyclomine eliminated the inconsolable crying of extreme fussiness, it would also prevent inattentive or emotionally distant parental behaviors described above. If parental behavior were the problem, we expected to find that infants successfully treated with dicyclomine would emerge from extreme fussiness with easier temperaments and fewer sleep disturbances than those infants who had received the placebo and kept on crying.

To our surprise, this was not the case. The infants in our study, each infant diagnosed as having extreme fussiness, did show the typical higher incidence of difficult temperament and sleep disturbances as compared to a normal population. But this was equally true of the infants successfully treated with dicyclomine and those who had received a placebo. In

other words, effective treatment for extreme fussiness symptoms did **not** alter later temperament ratings or sleep patterns when the infants were four months old.

This led us to conclude that difficult temperament and
briefer sleep duration in babies over four months of age who
had been extremely fussy infants under four months of age
does not result from the parents' response to extreme fussiness crying. Many of the babies in our study had their crying greatly reduced or almost eliminated by the drug, and
they still showed a higher-than-average incidence of difficult
to manage behaviors and sleep problems.

So it would seem that parents are not more to blame for a
four-month-old's brief sleep durations than they were to
blame for his crying as an extremely fussy two-month-old.
Instead, we believe that extreme fussiness, difficult temperament, and sleep disorders all share an underlying physical
cause. They are all manifestations of the same problem—
neurological, respiratory, endocrine and the like. Much more
research is needed to determine what is the source of the extreme fussiness-temperament-sleep triangle, but at least we
can feel confident in absolving parents of responsibility for
the symptoms.

This does not mean, of course, that your response to your
child's behavior has no effect. You can keep a tendency toward difficult temperament from growing into a long-term
behavioral problem. You can teach a child with brief sleep
durations to sleep longer and more soundly. Your attitude
can make extreme fussiness more or less bearable. The rest of
this book is designed to help you learn how to do this.

# II

# HOW TO SOOTHE YOUR NEWBORN: CARE, NOT CURE

# 8

## Soothing, Comforting, & Caring For Your Newborn

What exactly is soothing? Soothing is to restore to a normally peaceful state. To soothe your newborn is to render her calm or quiet; to bring her to a composed condition. We are attempting to establish a peaceful state of tranquility by reducing the force or intensity of fussiness. Our goal is to soften, tune down, or render less harsh the fussiness or crying. Soothing is pacifying or calming. We want to bring comfort to our baby; to bring a cessation of the agitation. At best, we hope to lull our baby into a relaxed sleepy state.

If fussiness is the natural byproduct of being born too early, then it is a stage of human development; it is not a disease. If it is not a disease state, then there is no 'cure.' This is why I think we should be attempting to find better ways to soothe, comfort, and care for our newborns' fussiness instead of searching for some medical remedy.

The bad news is that there is at present no sure-fire way to avoid fussiness. The good news is that there are ways to manage extreme fussiness until it goes away of its own accord when your baby is between three to four months of age.

You have already taken several important steps. You have learned all you can about extreme fussiness. You have identified fallacies and old wives' tales. You have stopped blaming yourself. You understand that extreme fussiness will not harm your baby and that it will come to an end. Here are some more concrete suggestions.

### Soothing Your Extremely Fussy Newborn

**Rhythmic motions** are the most effective method of soothing your infant. Use a cradle, rocking chair, baby swing, or 'snuggly'; take the baby for automobile rides or simply walk with him. Rocking motions may be gentle movements or vigorous swinging, depending on what your child responds to. Jiggling or bouncing may calm your baby. Some parents claim that raising and lowering the baby like an elevator ride is effective. Perhaps these rhythmic movements are comforting because they are similar to what a baby feels before he is born.

**Gentle pressure** such as experienced when embraced or hugged makes us feel good. Swaddling or gentle wrapping, sleeping in a car seat, or being held in a soft baby carrier or sling are other ways to exert gentle pressure. Here too, perhaps the sensation of gentle pressure resembles a state of comfort that the baby feels before he is born. Both rhythmic motions and gentle pressure may be effective because human babies are born too early. This was previously discussed under the concept of 'exterogestation.' If correct, then it is likely that rhythmic motions and gentle pressure exert their soothing effects because they partially re-create the sensations that the baby felt in the womb.

Recently there has been talk about **"baby massage"** as a way to calm extremely fussy babies.

Massaging babies has been observed in many different cultures and has a long history. It is not just a new fad. One particular benefit from massaging your newborn is that the mother or father directly benefits from this activity. While lovingly stroking your baby, you smile at your baby, talk softly, or you might sing or hum. These efforts, while focused on your baby, also relax you! Since fathers cannot breast feed their babies, I encourage them to develop an intimate bond with their newborn by practicing baby massage right away. Even before any fussiness begins. Use a natural cold-pressed fruit or vegetable oil. You gently stroke the skin and gently knead your baby's muscles. All the movements are gently performed. Books with pictures and videos are available to assist you. Baby massage is not a gimmick or a cure of extreme fussiness. However, it does soothe babies. Equally important, it provides you with a singular opportunity to be completely focused on your baby. Turn off the phones and pagers. You are doing something quite different from feeding, changing, and bathing. Comforting your baby this way will give you an inner calmness which will help you get through possible rough times when your baby is extremely fussy and not very soothable.

**Sucking** is soothing. Sometimes a pacifier, a finger, wrist, fist, or bottle temporarily calms the baby. Do not assume that when your baby eagerly takes a bottle he is necessarily hungry. Many extremely fussy babies suck more liquid than they need and spit up much of what they swallowed. If you are nursing, remember that just because a bottle of formula or water calms your baby, this does not mean that there is a nursing problem. When babies are fussy, they often behave as if they are hungry because sucking is soothing. During non-nutritive sucking, the baby does not suck in a steady rhythmic manner as he does when he is hungry; instead, he starts and stops, twists and turns. He is fussy.

Be careful, however, not to bombard your baby with stimuli. Initially, try to appeal to one sense at a time: tactile (massaging, rubbing, kissing, rocking, patting, changing from hip to shoulder), auditory (singing, humming, playing lullabies, running the vacuum cleaner), sight (bright lights, mobiles, television), or rhythmic motion (swings, cradles, car rides, going for a walk). Sometimes, doing too many of these things simultaneously or with too much force has a stimulating rather than a relaxing effect. However, if your baby remains fussy, try combinations of these different modalities.

Try to synchronize your actions with your baby's rhythms. If he is tense, taut, with deep exhausted heaving sobs and little physical movement, try rubbing his back ever so gently or moving your cheek over his in a slow rhythm which coincides with his breathing pattern. If he is boxing with his fists, jerking his legs and arching his back, maybe a ride on your shoulders will grab his attention and arrest the spell. You will find that after a while you become attuned to nuances within your baby's rhythms and respond accordingly.

### Useless Remedies

Be skeptical about the supposed miracles accomplished with crib vibrators, hot water bottles, herbal teas, or recordings of heart beat or womb sounds. There has been a great deal of nonsense written about burping techniques, nipple sizes and nipple shapes, baby bottle straws, feeding and sleep positions, lamb's wool pads, diets for nursing mothers, special formulas, pacifiers and solid food. These items have nothing to do with extreme fussiness, crying, temperament, or sleeping habits.

Many useless remedies can be purchased without a prescription. Anti-gas drops have never been shown to be more effective than a placebo in well conducted studies. One popular pellet contains chamomile, calcium phosphate, coffee, and a very small amount of active belladonna chemicals (0.0000095 percent). Another remedy contains natural blackberry flavor, Jamaica ginger, oil of anise, oil of nutmeg, and 2 percent alcohol. Maybe enough alcohol will sedate some infants! Please read labels carefully—any natural substance, flavoring agent or herb might have pharmacological effects. Call a school of pharmacy or a medical school to find experts in pharmagnosy, the study of natural herbs and plants, to find out if a particular plant or herb is dangerous.

Beware of gimmicks. Deaths of newborns have occurred when they drowned in rocking waterbeds, when they strangulated by having their necks overhang a trampoline-like crib platform, when the suffocated by burying their heads into pillows. Beware of prescribed drugs. The London Times headline of May 22, 1998 screamed "Baby died after drop of medicine for wind." A midwife "diagnosed trapped wind" and prescribed what was thought to be peppermint water.

Also be cautious in using home remedies. One mother almost killed her baby by giving a mixture of Morton's Salt Substitute with lactobacillus acidophilus culture, as prescribed in the popular book, *Let's Have Healthy Children*, by Adelle Davis.

### Everything Works . . . for a While

When you believe that something is going to calm your baby—herbal tea, womb recordings, lamb's wool blankets, you name it—often it appears to work, for a while. You are emotionally expecting relief because you trust the advice of an authority. Your fatigue may breed inflated hopes for a cure, and the day by day variability in infant crying creates the illusion that a particular remedy works, but only for a while. What really is happening is a placebo effect; this is the emotional equivalent of an optical illusion.

Mothers may fool themselves into believing that their baby is better because of a new formula or special tea. Of course, reality sets in after a few days and shatters the illusion. Some mothers sincerely believe that their babies habituate to, or become accustomed to, the benefits from the new formula or tea much like the dope addict needs increased doses to produce the desired feeling. Some doctors believe the mother's reports and agree that the babies really did improve for a day or two because the babies received novel stimulation.

Novelty is unlikely to be important because parents report that upon reintroduction, weeks after the special tea or gimmick was discarded, they see no improvement. In other words, there was no placebo effect the second time around. Naturally, if the baby coincidentally outgrows extreme fussiness when a useless remedy is introduced, the mother, the family, and even the doctor might become convinced that the useless remedy actually cured the extreme fussiness!

## Nightlights

If your baby cries at night, darken his room. Infants are not afraid of the dark. Extreme fussiness is not the expression of bad dreams. A light burning in a closet or even a conventional seven-watt nightlight can keep a sensitive baby from sleeping well. If you were absolutely convinced that your baby would not sleep in a totally black room, I would suggest using a guide light (quarter watt), which produces a faint yellow glow.

### Feeding Your Extremely Fussy Baby

Keep reminding yourself that extreme fussiness is not indigestion. It is not caused by formula or breast milk. Switching from one formula to the other will not help stop the crying. Some manufacturers of infant formulas try to sell their product by claiming that their product will reduce fussiness. The so-called research they cite to support their claims is weak, unconvincing, and has not been reproduced.

If you are nursing and fear your baby is crying from hunger—nearly all nursing mothers wonder at times if they have enough milk—arrange to have the baby weighed at a doctor's office several times over the course of a week or two. Chances are you will find her gaining weight nicely.

Do not let extreme fussiness make you give up breast-feeding if you want to continue. Your baby is still getting all the benefits of breast milk, even if she seems at times not to appreciate them. If you stick with it, you can look forward to many calm, pleasant months of nursing once the extreme fussiness has run its course.

Still, nursing an extremely fussy baby is undeniably a challenge. When nursing, infants with extreme fussiness tend to be gulpers, twisters, and forceful suckers. Sometimes they seem to reject the breast entirely. The determined nursing mother is in a bind; it is difficult to nurse a tense, twisting infant, but this is one of the few maneuvers that appear to calm the child (at least temporarily). The mother finds herself nursing very often—either because she interprets the extreme fussiness as hunger cries or simply to get some peace. She is often rewarded with painful, cracked nipples and/or exhaustion. Non-nutritive nursing, using your breasts as pacifiers, may calm baby but it is no picnic for mother! Here is a description of the nursing predicament by the mother of one of my young patients:

> The first three weeks of Michael's life led me to believe that having a baby would be a breeze. His behavior was almost identical from day to day. He was very calm, and so were my husband and I. Michael would eat—breastfeeding about eight to ten minutes on each side. He had no problems burping after each meal. Then I'd either hold him a while, lay him on his back, and talk or play with him. The usual schedule from the time he got up until he went to sleep would be one to one and half-hours. He would usually sleep anywhere from two and a half to four hours. Everyone would say to me, "Boy, are you ever lucky to have such a good baby."
>
> As the fourth week approached, Michael's behavior changed drastically. He no longer wanted to sleep during the day. I felt like all he wanted was my breast. I concluded that he either was continually hungry or had strong sucking needs.
>
> By the middle of each afternoon I was exhausted. Almost every hour I found myself breastfeeding. Sometimes I could put him off for two hours, but he'd cry a lot. I'd change his diaper, walk him, hold him, rock him, sing to him, change his position and so on. Nothing would please him except my breast, which was terribly tiring, to say the least. The thing that saved our lives is that he slept long hours through the night—probably because he was exhausted from being up all day. The worst times were midafternoon, and again between 5:00

P.M. and 10:00 P.M., after which he would sleep for around five hours straight. He would fuss and cry and nothing would calm him except when he was nursing.

If you are in a predicament similar to this mother's give yourself some relief by trying the following suggestions:

1. Space feedings a few hours apart. One mother said, "I must have Chinese' breast milk; he gets hungry just one hour after nursing." If you last nursed your baby well less than two hours ago (not a snack or a sip), he has no room in his stomach for more milk and your breasts contain little or no milk for him. Nursing too frequently is pointless, and if it causes you pain or exhaustion, it is destructive. See if your baby will accept a pacifier instead.

2. Ask your doctor about hydrocortisone ointment. A famous pediatric dermatologist at the Children's Memorial Hospital who nursed her own children suggests treating cracked nipples with one-percent hydrocortisone ointment. It is safe for mother and baby, and seems to work better than any other treatment. Many of my patient's mothers have reported rapid healing of sore nipples by using this treatment: After nursing, allow your breasts to air dry. Then, apply a thin film of the one per cent hydrocortisone ointment to the dry or cracked areas. Make sure that you use ointment, not cream because a cream might cause a painful burning sensation. When you are about to nurse again, do not wipe off or wash off any of the ointment. Most of it will have been absorbed into your breast skin and the small amount that your baby will absorb will cause no harm. Basically, the skin of the breast can become very dry, cracked or fissured from being wet or damp for prolonged periods of time. This inflammation is being treated with the hydrocortisone.

3. Don't exhaust yourself. One mother of an extremely fussy infant stored breast milk so that her husband could feed the baby once during the night and her mother could handle a similar daytime feeding. In this way she was able to get some extra rest. When the baby was several weeks old, the baby's grandmother went home and the father returned to work. Now, all alone and very busy, the mother saw her previously ample supply of breast milk dwindle to almost nothing. We discussed how she had decreased her fluid intake, how she was worried about her mother's departure and generally under strain. I reassured her that while it was important to continue having the child suck at her breasts to stimulate milk production, a single bottle of formula for one or two days would not harm the baby or inhibit lactation. She increased her fluid intake, rested more, and after four to five days was again nursing with more than ample milk production. Throughout this period the child continued to have severe extreme fussiness spells with periods of inconsolable crying. This mother knew that the crying was not related to nursing.

Another mother of one of my patients felt especially bad when nursing failed to calm her baby:

It's early evening and my daughter is screaming and restless. Nothing seems to calm her, not even nursing. I didn't think Chelsea was colicky but she sure was fussy. Although her fussiness wasn't any everyday occurrence, it persisted from her second or third week of life until about two months of age.

At first I thought something I was eating was causing her to have gas. Then I felt her behavior was due to my inexperience as a mother. As these episodes continued, I began to feel inadequate, desperate, sad and exhausted.

I felt inadequate as a parent. I didn't know what to do to comfort my child, or whether what I was doing was right. I especially felt inadequate when Chelsea rejected my breast. It seemed as if nothing could console and comfort her.

We had visions of a child who could be comforted at the touch of her mom or dad. Soon all the sleepless nights and exaggerated feelings of incompetency led to exhaustion. Would this cycle ever end? Well, it finally did. With the help of our pediatrician, we soon began to realize that this behavior was normal and would not last indefinitely. I also found that her fussiness was neither caused nor enhanced by my behavior. Along with this realization came the light at the end of the tunnel. I then knew her fussiness would not last forever.

I became aware of certain behavioral changes that manifested themselves either before or after each fussy period. She would startle easily, have difficulty falling asleep and then would sleep for shorter periods of time. Also, during her fussy periods she exhibited different behavioral characteristics. She was restless and would scream with a quivering chin. She would become stiff or have rigid movements. She would not nurse, or when she did she would suck frantically. She would become overtired but would not sleep. Sometimes she would be wide-awake one moment and sound asleep a second later.

Chelsea is now three months old. Her fussy periods have ceased and she wakes in the morning with a smile that lasts all day. We really love our "perfect" child.

Sometimes a nursing mother notices that the baby seems calmer in her husband's arms than in her own. She may feel that her husband does a better job of soothing the baby, that perhaps the baby "prefers" him to her. What is really happening is quite simple. The baby recognizes that his mother is the source of milk. When she holds him he quite naturally squirms and twists, rooting around, looking to suck, even when he is not hungry.

I want to encourage every mother's desire to nurse her extremely fussy baby. It is an important accomplishment for both of them. One mother called me when her extremely fussy baby was exactly three months old. She was determined to continue nursing and to start working part-time. Her husband was a fireman and found it very difficult to be around his crying baby on days off. She was under enormous stress. All her friends claimed that if she would feed her baby formula, then the crying would disappear. She wanted to—and did—keep on nursing after the extreme fussiness disappeared to show them, and herself, that nursing was not the cause of the crying. Here is a report from the mother of another one of my patients; persevering with nursing helped her maintain her confidence and self-esteem:

> Both my husband and I questioned our best judgments and our ability to care for Lisa. At one point I questioned my ability to nurse and felt that I was literally poisoning my baby. Her screaming episodes came a predictable ten minutes after every feeding. At times I felt tortured. I consider myself a rational and caring person, yet often found myself crying in the shower or praying that my husband could somehow relieve the tension, anger, and helplessness that I felt.
>
> At *six* weeks, Lisa seemed to be easing into patterns and appeared finally to be getting good, deep sleep. Her smiling times were numerous, but she still had hours of screaming. I overcame my fear of nursing and decided to continue weeks after I had planned to stop. Nursing became the one pleasurable experience the baby and I had together. When I finally did wean Lisa it was a sad time; we were separate after being together for so long.

*Six weeks of age or six weeks after the due date* is truly a magic turning point for many babies.

*Your Relationship With Your Extremely Fussy Baby*

Extreme fussiness strikes during the early months when the parent-child relationship is just forming. Daily bouts of screaming, with the attendant guilt and worry, can, of course, interfere with this relationship. You must keep reminding yourself that although your baby is in distress, he is not rejecting you or commenting on your ability as a parent.

Parents should be especially aware of their behavior toward their baby during the first few months, particularly when the baby is calm and alert and social interaction is possible. These times will become more frequent as your baby approaches his three-month birthday, and should be taken advantage of. Although your behavior may not have a dramatic effect on extreme fussiness, it will have an accumulative effect in the sense that you're learning a way of responding to your child. If you tend to respond in a tense, anxious manner, even when your baby isn't crying, this not only robs you of enjoying those "good" times, but also can influence your baby's behavior when the bout with extreme fussiness is over. When your baby is fussy, drowsy, or both, he is almost out of reach. If your baby cries when awake and/or doesn't rest well when asleep, he is probably not going to be very sociable, attentive, or receptive to the messages you send him. It is crucial that you shower your baby with attention during those times when he is awake and not crying, and prepare for a burst of interaction as soon as the extreme fussiness goes away.

Do not let the extreme fussiness throw you off balance. Love your crybaby all the time. If you are able to respond calmly, you will be able to enjoy your baby more during the non-fussy periods and your baby will enjoy you more. When a baby's extreme fussiness behavior adversely affects the mother's behavior; they can reinforce each other's distress. Remember to treat your infant in the same loving way whether he is crying or content. How the child's temperament and sleeping patterns will ultimately turn out are probably related more to your behavior during this time than to the original physiologic disturbance(s) that caused the extreme fussiness.

### Take Care of Yourself

An extremely fussy baby needs a great deal of attention. You may find your life filled with rocking, walking, feeding, and soothing. But the truth is, most of what you will be doing about the extreme fussiness is waiting it out. Try to keep up your health, good cheer, and loving relationships during this difficult time. Don't forget about yourself, and the rest of your family. Then you will all be ready to give the baby your best love and care.

It is normal for parents to be angry, bewildered, frustrated and guilty about feeling that way. Resolve to break that circle right now. You have had an unlucky break and you are entitled to feel resentful sometimes. Maintaining a sense of humor is hard, but any mother with an extremely fussy infant will feel better getting her feelings out into the open.

Whenever possible, the mother should have her husband, friends, or babysitter take over care of the screamer so that she can get away. If you feel reluctant, remember that your baby's crying will not be as bothersome to a "stranger" as it is to you, his mother. This is not self-indulgence—you must have frequent breaks from your extremely fussy baby. Fathers should plan to come home early or take a few days off when the baby is about six weeks old in order to give mothers a much-deserved break. Mothers, I know that you may feel reluctant to ask your hard-working husband to take your baby for a late night car ride after putting in a full day at the office. But remember this, no matter how hard his work is he is able to take some breaks; if you have a newborn with extreme fussiness, you have taken no breaks! Call it tag-team parenting or one-on-one defense if you have only one child. If you have more than one child, call it zone defense!

As we have seen from studies on crying, responding promptly and consistently when a baby under three months cries is better than waiting to see if he settles down. He probably won't, and the time you spend waiting and listening is unpleasant for you. On the other hand, if none of your efforts seem to calm the baby, it is not necessary to exhaust yourself. If you run out of energy, you are now totally exhausted, you are at your wits end, and you find he is as unhappy in your arms as in his crib, then put him down and let him cry. A baby in the midst of a truly inconsolable spell of extreme fussiness probably does not know whether he is being held or not. Talking a break from the continuous fussiness/crying before you break down is being smart, not selfish. Remember that you are the source of your newborn's comfort and sometimes you have to rest to recharge our battery so that you can continue to comfort your baby.

A popular recommendation is to try for fifteen or twenty minutes to soothe the child; if you see no results, put him down for about half an hour and then try again. In my experience, most mothers are able to, and want to, spend more than twenty minutes soothing their babies but are not willing to endure even half an hour of crying.

> Can a mother sit and hear
> An infant groan, an infant fear?
> No, no! Never can it be!
> Never, never can it be!
>                    William Blake

Spend as much time as you can with your baby, but do not feel compelled to spend six or eight solid hours consoling him without a break. Many fathers have experienced the pleasure of automobile rides at three in the morning with their baby to give their wives a break. Fathers quickly learn how hard it is to be a loving parent and husband while always on the verge of falling asleep.

### Creative Parenting

I believe that over the long run, creative parenting behavior will override whatever temporary disturbances are

causing extreme fussiness. The problem is that some parents—especially mothers—become so distraught or fatigued
that it prevents calm, thought-out parenting. Conflict can
erupt among family members over how to handle the problem. Husband and wife may expend energy blaming each
other. Everyone's self-esteem can suffer, and no one will have
the resourcefulness to try strategies that might end up helping. So try to get enough rest, keep your wits about you, and
get away for occasional quiet evenings. Whatever works, do
it. Wear your baby in a sling, sleep with your baby, and use
gentle rhythmic motion to help your newborn sleep. Use different ways to hold or cuddle with your newborn.

### Hospitalization

In the past, extremely fussy babies were sometimes
hospitalized. Frankly, this was done because some doctors
believed that extreme fussiness results from a family situation
that more or less drove the baby crazy. Today, of course, we
know that this is not true. Still, a doctor will occasionally
propose to remove a baby from the family for awhile, for
"tests and observation." You should know that as long as
the baby is gaining weight and exhibits no abnormalities
apart from the extreme fussiness symptoms discussed in this
book, hospitalization would not accomplish anything. The
real motive is to give the parents some relief.

If a doctor should suggest hospitalizing your severely extreme fussiness infant, talk with her very frankly. Does she
have a real reason to believe the problem is something more
than extreme fussiness? Exactly what tests will be performed
and what can he learn from them? Why does she feel your
baby should be separated from you? What can be learned
from "observing" the baby in the hospital rather than at
home? You should probably get a second opinion before even
considering this drastic move.

I believe that hospitalization for extreme fussiness is never
justified. It is very expensive, and infants can easily catch serious infections in hospitals. Having a baby in the hospital is

extremely stressful on parents and it can be upsetting to the baby. Even if your baby's extreme fussiness is so bad that the idea of respite looks good to you, there are many cheaper, safer alternatives: hire a full-time sitter, or even a private-duty nurse; go to a hotel for the weekend; alternate with your husband spending nights away from home; leave the baby with relatives for a day or two.

Remember that many, many parents have lived through extreme fussiness. It is a trying experience, but does not really last all that long. Your extremely fussy baby—even if her crying is very persistent and very severe—is not sick and does not belong in a hospital. She belongs at home with people who love her.

### Caring For a Family With an Extremely Fussy Newborn

Caring for a family is different from treating or 'managing' extreme fussiness in a newborn. 'Treatment' implies the presence of a medical problem that if treated or managed correctly will be solved and health restored. There is no good evidence that extremely fussy newborns are unhealthy or are suffering from a medical problem. Fussiness appears to be a pre-cry state. That is, if the fussiness is unattended, crying usually follows. The more skillful you become, the more effort you are able to put forth, and the earlier you start to soothe your baby, the less likely fussiness will escalate into crying. In other words, skillful soothing of fussiness may prevent much crying.

Prevention of extreme fussiness will be possible when the cause or causes are known. Based on my experience, the first step is to prevent unnecessary guilt, worry, and confusion on the part of the parents. The better they understand the nature of extreme fussiness, the better off they will be. I believe that the family should be prepared to cope with fussiness at the prenatal visit or first encounter after delivery with the pediatrician. Parents should be alerted before the birth of their child that extreme fussiness might occur and that steps can be taken if it does. I would recommend that parents ask about extreme fussiness even if the pediatrician does not bring up the subject. This is not borrowing trouble; it is being prepared.

All of the tips for living with extreme fussiness given in this chapter have helped large numbers of parents. The extreme fussiness months can be made bearable. Future behavioral and sleeping problems can be minimized. Nothing is more important to parents than a good dose of optimism; extreme fussiness does disappear. Parents will sleep again, as you'll learn through the experiences of several mothers of extremely fussy infants, some successful and some less successful, in later chapters.

# 9

## As Extreme
## Fussiness Ends

Through draggy afternoons, arsenic evenings, and long nights you have sometimes thought extreme fussiness would go on forever. But, eventually, when the baby is around three or four months old, you should begin to notice a let-up in the fussing/crying. The baby may be more able to be soothed, skip days of crying, may have fewer spells, or briefer ones. The change in her behavior may be abrupt and dramatic, or it may be gradual and erratic. After months of disappointment with temporary "improvement" cruelly followed by even worse relapses, you may not dare believe what is happening. But one day you will say to your husband or he to you, "You know, she really is a lot better."

This is certainly a time for celebration. You have lived through extreme fussiness, but you may not have reached the Promised Land yet. Sometimes a miracle does occur, and within days the baby becomes quiet, cheerful, relaxed, and a good sleeper. Other children, however, do indeed cry less but they remain irritable and hard to soothe, and awaken easily from sleep because they have become very over-tired. With careful handling, you may be able to prevent the over-tired state before it becomes serious.

### Time For a Change

During the extreme fussiness period, your child has learned to associate falling asleep with specific behaviors such as extended rocking, walking, hugging, and feeding. She comes to expect this attention when she drifts off to sleep. The process of falling asleep is learned behavior. She may never have learned to fall asleep by herself. She may be, in a sense, addicted to social interaction in order to fall asleep. When older, after three or four months of age, some of these babies develop an over-tired state because they are receiving less of this soothing attention or the parents fail to establish healthy sleep habits. So even after the physiological causes of the crying (whatever they are) have abated, the old fussy pattern might remain.

Parents, too, become conditioned after several months of coping with extreme fussiness. They have grown used to lavishing prompt, continual attention on their crying baby. The variable nature of extreme fussiness has taught them to shift strategies frequently. They have become improvisers—trying what worked last night, trying what worked this morning, or trying something new. It has never been practical for them to have a plan; they just responded. However, a baby who once was extremely fussy needs consistent, thought-out management to curtail bad habits. Parents must make a transition, too.

### A Gradual Approach

I would like to describe a gradual approach to be tried in infants three, four, or five months old, right after the extreme fussiness seems to have eased.

These are sensitive months in the development of a baby's crying and sleep patterns. In infants under three to four months, crying comes directly out of biological needs—for food and fluid, dry skin, contact and comfort, and in the case of extreme fussiness, for relief from the unknown causes. Babies this young will not be spoiled or taught bad habits by your response to their crying. Infants over four to six months old, by contrast, can indeed learn to cry in order to get their parents to do certain things. They have learned to cry for attention. And they may have learned how to keep themselves from falling asleep. These interim ages—three to six months—are a time to keep bad habits from forming and a promising time to teach a previously extreme fussiness, potentially sleepless baby how to stop crying and get enough rest. Remember that parents should be teachers!

### *The "Fade-Out" Procedure*

Basically, you will gradually decrease the amount of work you do when you put your baby to sleep. The goal is to let him develop internal resources to fall asleep. At the same time, you will be teaching yourself how to be the parents of a normal baby who does not always need your immediate attention.

Each family is different. Babies become ready at different ages. Please think of these suggestions as general principles rather than rigid rules. But do try to understand the basic theory: gradually, consistently cut back on the elaborate procedure you go through to get your child to sleep, until he is "weaned" from your company, so he can do it on his own.

### Step 1: Don't Pick Him Up

Your baby is now three to four months old. His extreme fussiness is not as bad as it once was, but he still awakens frequently at night. Begin by figuring out how often your baby is truly hungry at night. Ask yourself how often he really sucks with enthusiasm. Listen to the quality of the crying—true hunger crying in the older infant has a sound all its own. Calculate how much time has passed since the last feeding: if it is less than two hours your baby could not possibly be hungry.

have decided how often you should feed
ıt, pick him up and feed him at those times
~~out do not pick~~ him up at any other times. This is the first
step: do not pick the baby up unless you are going to feed
him.

Do you just ignore his cries? No. Go into his room and sit
beside him. Pat him, stroke him, or hold his hand. Let him
see you, and let him see you looking at him. Talk or sing.
Keep it calm and gentle. Stay beside him as long as necessary,
even until he falls asleep. Respond promptly each time he
cries—but do not pick him up unless it is time for feeding.

If your baby persists with inconsolable screaming despite
your soothing efforts, stop. Go back to what method(s) you
were using before. Try this suggestion again in a few weeks.
Once you are able to calm him down, and pick him up only
for feeding, move on to Step 2.

**Step 2: Cut Back on Your Responses**

Begin to cut back on what you do as you sit beside your
baby. You might give up the eye contact first, keeping the
room black and staying out of view. Later, stop rocking the
crib or stroking the baby. Go slowly and see what works.
The goal to be reached after a week or two is to reach the
stage where you are merely resting your hand on the baby's
back or quietly holding his hand. You still respond promptly
and take as much time as necessary to lull him into a deep
sleep. Pay attention to how much time this usually takes, and
proceed to Step 3.

**Step 3: Spend Less Time**

Try to reduce, by a minute or two at a time, the amount of
time you sit with your baby. Respond promptly, but slip away
a little sooner. If you find that he startles and cries when you
leave, go right back. After several days or a few weeks, you
may find that just putting your hand on his tummy or back
for a few minutes magically induces sleep. That will be a good

accomplishment: You will have loosened tl
baby used to make between long, complex
and falling asleep. Now he may do it with .....y .. q...... ....
surance of your presence.

## Step 4: Wait A While

Now, for the first time, wait a bit before you go to the
baby. Give him a chance to settle down by himself. Do not
wait so long that a full crying storm develops, for then he will
need a lengthy calming down. Wait two or three minutes to
start, wait longer when you feel you can. Learn to recognize
the drowsy, testing cries and wait them out. Your reward will
come on those nights when you hear a call, some whimpering, a faint cry, and then silence.

### *Will It Work?*

You need not take all these steps. If, for example, you
had success with Steps 1, 2, and 3, but find that your baby always develops crying fits when you try Step 4 stop where you
are. You have already made fine progress. Live with those
brief nocturnal visits a few months more until the child outgrows this dependence on your presence. Sometimes this
procedure works only when the father responds to the night
awakenings and proceeds through Steps 1 through 4.

If this plan does not work at all for you, make sure you
and your husband, and whoever else might tend to the baby
at night, are all being consistent. You should always know
how you plan to deal with the baby at night and you should
not give in, for example, pick him up, "just this once." It is
also possible that your child is not ready; try again in a few
weeks. I cannot predict whether this "fade-out procedure"
will work for a particular family, but it is based on tested
principles and I feel certain it is worth a serious try.

### 'Focus On The Morning Nap'

When three to six months old, try to establish a morning nap. The reason that you will focus on the morning nap is because a regular and long morning nap develops before an afternoon nap. Also, you are more likely to be successful for the morning nap because your baby is more rested in the morning following a night's sleep. Here we go.

First, keep the entire wakeful period from the end of the night to the beginning of the nap to no more than one hour. This ultra-short period of wakefulness helps prevent the over-tired state. Declare when you think the night sleep has ended: 5,6,7 A.M. and then look at your watch. Within one hour you clean, change, feed, and soothe back to sleep. This means that there is really no time or little time for playing. If you have bright natural light in your home, exposing him to bright natural light might help. Morning light seems to help set biological rhythms and help regulate sleeping patterns.

Second, after soothing for only several minutes, which may include breast-feeding or bottle-feeding, put your child down in his crib. At this particular moment, he may be asleep, awake, or in an in-between state. You don't care; you put him down. Your custom in the past may have been to always hold him until he was in a deep sleep state because you observed that if you put him down awake or in a twilight state he always cried hard. Now that he is three to six months old, his sleep rhythms are more developed. This means that you can use his natural or internal rhythm as an aid to help him fall asleep. This occurs if, and only if, you are synchronizing your putting down to sleep with the surfacing time of drowsiness. Just as a wave surfaces, the surfer will have a smooth ride only if he has good timing to catch the wave; your baby will smoothly fall asleep if you catch the drowsy wave.

So when you put your baby down, after soothing, sometimes he is not in a deep sleep state. This is the beginning of allowing your baby to develop some self-soothing skills. You are beginning to wean him from the expectation that you will always lull him into a deep sleep state.

Third, when you put him down, if he cries, ignore the crying for 5-10 minutes, maybe less, maybe more. Listen to your heart, is it a loud cry or a quiet whimper. The point is, you do not immediately pick up your baby when he cries. If, after crying, you pick him up, then you have two choices. One. The crying may have been so stressful to you that you go out with your baby for a walk to relax, calm down, and try it again the next morning. Two. Your baby is now falling asleep in your arms because you have picked him up and you decide to put him back down to see if he will stay asleep to take a nap.

Once the morning nap is established, try this procedure for subsequent naps. Keep the interval of wakefulness between the naps to a maximum of two hours. Within two hours, babies quickly become overtired and then it is difficult for them to fall asleep. The reason that the overtired state messes up good sleeping is that when you are overtired, the body's adaptive biological response to fight the fatigue by producing stimulating chemicals. This 'second wind' was important for early man's survival to continue to hunt, to fight, or to flee. But this 'second wind' interferes with the ability to fall asleep and stay asleep.

By three to six months of age, your baby will be taking a morning nap that starts between 9 and 10 A.M. and an afternoon nap that starts between 12 and 2 P.M. Each nap will last about one to two hours. The quality of sleep is probably better if it is motionless sleep in these older babies. The movement in strollers, swings, and cars might prevent them from getting the full restorative power of long deep sleep states.

### *"Do I Have To Put My Baby Down While She Is Still Awake?"*

No. No. No. Consistency in your style of soothing to sleep is important so that your child associates certain behaviors on your part with falling asleep. Extremely fussy newborns often settle down and drift off to sleep best when sucking breast or bottle. There are two common methods or soothing styles for lulling your child asleep. Method A is soothing for several minutes only, soothing may include feeding, then put your baby down whether he is or is not yet asleep. This rarely works for extremely fussy newborns under three months of age. Method B is soothing as long as is required for the newborn to drift into a deep sleep state and soothing usually includes feeding. This is the method used by most parents of extremely fussy newborns. What I am talking about here is how to put your baby asleep for naps and for night.

A totally separate issue is what to do when you hear your baby cry in the middle of the night. Between three and six months of age, extreme fussiness decreases and your baby is more able to sleep at night. Let's consider two approaches for these older infants.

At night, if your baby is in a bassinet or crib, plan to feed your baby once or twice, but not more than two times. The first is in the middle of the night and the second is early in the morning. You might even bring your baby into your bed for the second feeding early in the morning. It's your choice. If you go more often, if you assume every sound is a hunger cry, then you will create a night waking habit. The night waking habit emerges because of the stimulation to wakefulness that occurs when you move him about in order to feed him. By ignoring these other cries, your baby will learn to return to sleep unassisted by you. By responding to all these cries, this learning process does not occur. How you put your child down to sleep at naps and at the beginning of night sleep has nothing to do with how well he sleeps at night. How well he sleeps at night depends on how well you can tell the difference between his need to be fed, which you always respond to, and other vocalizations, which you ignore.

At night, if you are sleeping with your baby and breast-feeding, then you might feed much more often throughout the night and never create a night waking habit. This is be-

cause your baby is barely awake at the ti
Mother's sleeping brain is exquisitely se
sounds.

So forcing mothers to put their child down to sleep when
their baby is awake not only does not make sense, it is contrary to what most mothers instinctively feel is right.

### As Extreme Fussiness Ends

1. Keep the intervals of wakefulness brief; no more
   than 2 hours.
2. Use motionless sleep.
3. Be consistent in soothing style.

# 10

## There Is Life After Extreme Fussiness

*Mothers' Descriptions of Their Babies at Age Four Months*

As part of a study on extremely fussy infants, I had the opportunity to study the parents' responses to the Infant Temperament Questionnaire, filled out when the infants were about four months old. Several mothers included a narrative account of the changes they had seen and I quote from these below. None of these infants was in my practice; I had not given any advice or counseling to these mothers. All the infants had extreme fussiness as defined by Wessel, and the extreme fussiness had disappeared by the time the parents filled out the questionnaire.

These comments from mothers of different backgrounds and circumstances illustrate the variety of ways extreme fussiness can resolve itself. As you read on, you will see that behavior during the extreme fussiness period makes babies appear as alike as peas in a pod. There is not much individuality among screaming babies, especially to their exhausted mothers. However, the children outgrow this awful period with vastly different temperaments. I hope you have a sweet baby at four months!

### "He's Come a Long Way"

"With the extreme fussiness months behind us, I find Jacob very enjoyable and really no problem at all. Jacob has really come a long way from two months ago. He went from being a crying, crabby baby to a basically happy baby. His routine is, for the most part, regular. He tends to be a bit cranky around the dinner hour, but is calmed with picking up or just being in the middle of the activity. He enjoys being right in the middle of everything and everyone, and is up quite a bit. He gets excited watching his brother and sister play. He gets really excited and laughs when he plays with daddy. If he's crabby and squirming, you know he's either wet or sleepy or it's time to eat. On the whole, I would say he is a fairly content little guy!"

### "He Became A New Baby"

"At almost three months to the day, I felt Daniel was over his extreme fussiness. He became a new baby with long times of playing and watching and seemed very happy. He suddenly established a routine of sleeping, eating and being awake. He followed it faithfully if my husband or me were the ones taking care of him. With anyone else, the routine of sleep was shortened and awake times lengthened, so he'd be fussy at the end, but it is amazing what a happy baby he has become. The only times that are still rather difficult are when he is in a car seat. When I hold him in the back of the van he is perfectly content. However, I drive a small car and then he in a car seat, which proves to be distressing. Daniel does not take a pacifier on his own and will spit it out unless I help hold it. Rarely does he keep the pacifier in for more than sixty seconds if he's fussy, and he does not suck his thumb or fingers in place of the pacifier. Before with extreme fussiness he needed constant attention and there was no solution to his crying. Now he is becoming a happy person. Fussiness now means specific problems: diaper, food, sleep, etc."

Daniel's mother, a thirty-two-year-old teacher, described her baby as not sucking very much. Brazelton reported that crying and sucking behavior were inversely related to each other. That is, crybabies do not suck very much and thumb suckers do not cry very much.

### "She Can Focus Her Energy Instead of Crying"

"Katherine's extreme fussiness varied widely from day to day. On a good day there might have been only two to three hours of mild fussiness in the evening. She took naps, sleeping perhaps four hours during the day. She always slept from midnight to 7:00 A.M. There were several play periods of twenty to forty minutes, and she certainly was fun! On bad days the extreme fussiness lasted from six to eight hours, most of it in the moderate category, maybe an hour or two really severe. On these days, she was unable to sleep during the day. She would fall asleep but awaken a few moments later. Holding, rocking, and the pacifier helped, but she was unusually jumpy. The sound of my breathing startled her, for example. She still had some play periods after eating, but they were much shorter and less frequent. I ended up holding her most of the day. In an average week she had three bad days. One of the fussy days was due to her first DPT shot. I also noticed that on bad days, she looked pale and there was some perspiration on her forehead before she began crying. I could sometimes tell ahead of time that she was going to have problems."

At about four months: "In general, Katie has had less severe extreme fussiness, fewer hours of extreme fussiness, and has slept more. It has been easier to get her to sleep and easier to keep her asleep. Her play periods are longer, and it's been interesting to watch her focus her energy on looking, reaching, batting and feeling things instead of having it tied up in crying. There has been only one instance of severe extreme fussiness since, and it was short. She still has some "jittery" times, but on the whole they seem less severe. She still tends to have at least one very active period in the evening during which she energetically leaps, smiles, frowns, coughs, burps, widens her eyes and so on. However, she is less apt to disintegrate into screaming. More often, she falls into a light sleep and the rapidly changing facial expressions and panting continue for a few moments. Then she either awakens in a quieter mood or goes into a sound sleep."

The comments regarding panting are interesting because many mothers noted that just prior to the onset of extreme fussiness the babies might breathe rapidly and with shallow respiration. Other mothers noted deep or labored breathing, like rapid sighs, just before the extreme fussiness occurred. These changes in breathing patterns were previously reported by Wessel. Perhaps smooth muscle contractions in the lung are causing increased resistance to breathing similar to what occurs in asthmatics. The comment regarding perspiration or pallor before the crying started had not been previously reported, but perspiration was noted in the following mother's report.

### "She Fights Sleep"

"My four-month-old infant, Marjorie, cries and fusses after her bath almost always for two to five minutes. She fights sleep continuously (one to two hours), rejects the last bottle, stiffens her body and when held pushes away from me by bending her legs, passing gas and her body perspires. Rocking, being held, played with, walked, etc. does not stop her shrill crying. The difficulty in the evenings has left me feeling that either she is spoiled or I'm not following a schedule properly and am promoting this overtired, extremely fussy period myself. Marjorie has been this way for ten weeks, but in the past six weeks she's become even more difficult to get to sleep."

### "Cries Herself to Sleep"

"Tai is strong-willed, yet usually agreeable. She laughs and smiles very easily and is not fearful of strangers. She generally has a very good disposition. She is very inquisitive and very vocal. Tai frequently moves her arms and legs vigorously when playing with toys. She is very affectionate and generally likes to be held. When tired and fighting sleep, Tai becomes much more difficult. Even when she falls asleep while nursing she usually awakens when put into her crib and cries vigorously [i.e., red face, with tears and perspiration] for five to fifteen minutes until she falls asleep. Tai rarely sleeps longer than four hours at a time. During the daytime, naps range from thirty minutes to two and a half-hours. She usually awakens from naps more calmly than she did a month or so ago. That is especially true if she has slept for a longer period of time.

"During the night, Tai usually sleeps for about four hours and awakens whimpering or crying. She is easily calmed by holding and nursing and falls asleep readily. When returned to her crib, however, she almost always cries for a few minutes before settling down to sleep. She does not cry if she is nursed in our bed and not moved."

### "Very Opinionated"

"Charles has definitely calmed down, but is still very active during the day. When extreme fussiness was bad, it was at its worst during the day, no matter what I did. He is very opinionated as to what he'll eat and has lost interest in his bottle already. He still gets spurts of gas once in a while."

*What Mothers Say About First Babies After Extreme Fussiness Ends*

Here are some young mothers describing their first-

born babies after they've grown out of a bout of extreme
fussiness.

## "He Doesn't Sleep Like Other Children"

"David is a happy boy in general. He loves to take baths
and kick in the tub. He also loves to have his hair brushed,
his body rubbed with lotion, nails cut, ears cleaned, nose
cleaned, etc. David is big on eating—anything he can suck—
he still sucks his thumb when sleeping. He loves to be put on
the changing table to dress and have his diaper changed. And
he loves to be talked to! He is very friendly towards everyone
and smiles and coos a lot. David is just great when we take
him out—stores, houses—loves all the new things. He is easily stimulated by sights and sounds. David still doesn't sleep
like other children, as long, that is, but he does sleep seven to
eight hours each night, and one hour in the morning and
one hour in the afternoon for naps, which sure beats being up
every two hours!"

## "I Feed Her Very Often"

"It is very hard, even impossible, to put Stephanie on a
feeding schedule. When I do feed my child she never eats.
I'm talking about nursing her more than ten minutes total, so
I don't think she's very full. I find myself feeding her frequently. She gets very, very angry sometimes and will scream,
and sometimes I can't tell if she might be in extreme pain."

## "Nights Are Still Difficult"

"Previously, Matthew's extreme fussiness could be described as moderate in nature with a total duration of about
six hours each day—usually three hours in the early morning
(3:00 A.M. to 7:00 A.M. or so), 11:00 A.M. to noon, and
4:00 P.M. to 6:00 P.M., and sometimes again between 9:00
P.M. and midnight. He usually had about ten wakings between midnight and 9:00 A.M. One rocking movement that

he often responded to when crying intensely was an elevator-like movement—up and down on his back. However, this is physically demanding and can't be done for long. Now, his general behavior pattern is characterized by pleasantness. Matthew smiles most of the day and maintains the ability to charm, play and coo. However, night wakings are continually a problem. For the last three weeks he has awakened every hour."

### "Demands a Lot of Attention"

"I have noticed marked improvements in Jonathan's behavior during his fourth month. Since his extreme fussiness pains have subsided, he seems to be enjoying what life has to offer. However, when he gets tired of a certain activity (play, bath, swing, etc.), he is very impatient and screams continuously until I pick him up and move on to something else. I can't coax him to stay with a task if he doesn't want to. He is at a point now where he is showing a lot of emotion. He smiles and giggles out loud for long periods of time but he can cry two minutes later because he wants a change of activity. Jonathan demands a lot of attention and I wonder if this is because of when he had extreme fussiness. Dinner is a difficult time because Jonathan does not like to sit and amuse himself while we eat. This is a problem we are still working on. Maybe this is true with many children. This being my first child, I'm not sure what is typical behavior but I would consider his temperament to be more difficult than average since he demands so much attention."

### "She's Usually Calmer"

"Annie has a generally sunny disposition and is extremely gregarious. She does have strong negative reactions to things she's not ready for like dressing or being put to bed. When she was younger, Annie seemed to overreact to stimulation and had many more fussy periods. She still reacts strongly, but not necessarily negatively, and is usually calm."

**"Dependency Is a Problem"**

"Nelida has a very high level of activity and expresses her emotions through her physical movements. She seems to prefer communication through body language rather than vocal expression. When she vocalizes it's more through a demanding cry rather than cooing and being pleasant. She's a very alert, attentive child with good concentration and attention span, especially when her energy is at its peak in the evening. Being with us makes her feel secure and it is essential for her becoming sociable and outgoing. This has developed into a problem because her attachment and dependency has developed to such a degree that Nelida refuses to develop independence, or allow us to have ours."

> *Second-born Infants Are Like First-borns After Extreme Fussiness Ends*
>
> Second born children who have had extreme fussiness are described in terms similar to those used by mothers of firstborn infants.

**"Requires a Lot of Sleep"**

"Elizabeth is only getting a formula for feedings—no solids. Four eight-ounce bottles keep her full. Her sleeping patterns and preferences are giving us the most problems. She requires a lot of sleep and is only awake six to seven hours a day. The problem is she will only sleep on her stomach in a crib. Sleeping in cribs other than her own also shortens her naps. She does not particularly enjoy stroller rides or car seats and never falls asleep in them. Her favorite activities involve being with other people. She enjoys being held, walked, talked to and played with. We are trying to encourage longer play periods alone. It's hard to take her places. She requires a lot of holding and walking."

### "No Two Days Alike"

"Scott's behavior varies from day to day. It seems there are never two days in a row that are alike. He does follow something of a schedule for eating and sleeping but his behavior during waking hours changes a lot. He can almost always be comforted by holding."

### "No Problem At All"

"At first, Nathaniel's crying was a problem because I didn't feel emotionally strong enough to handle it. A three-month span of extreme fussiness seemed like it would be forever to me. We had trouble taking him visiting because right after suppertime (about 7:30 P.M.) he would start to cry and wouldn't quit. No one could understand why he would suck a bottle and scream like it was hurting him. Once he got wound up he had a hard time relaxing and calming down. Now his temperament is no problem at all. I enjoy him. I think he's a cute baby. Maybe I'll have a third sometime!"

### "I Can See More and More How to Help Her"

"Although Lauren has greatly improved since the time of her extreme fussiness, she can't relax in her environment. If she ever must wait for something, especially a nap or feeding she will begin by fussing and then dissolve into tears. If this occurs around naptime she will take about twenty minutes to settle herself down, during which time there must be no stimulation at all. If she fusses at feeding time she will generally refuse the breast. The only solution is to place her in the crib and let her cry it out, the end result being a short nap, after which she wakes up cheerful and ready to eat."

"However, Lauren more than makes up for these angry outbursts by being a very responsive child. She smiles a lot, freely giving belly laughs. She especially loves playing with her older sister and me. She can maintain cheerful play for up to an hour and sometimes more after a feeding. Her motor development is very good. One thing I've noticed is that she doesn't sleep well anywhere but in her own crib—she's very aware of changes in bed. For example, she won't fall asleep in a restaurant in a car bed, but she can sometimes sleep in a snuggly. It feels good to see the light at the end of the tunnel. I can see more and more how to help Lauren over her sometimes very difficult irritability. I'm feeling much better about our relationship."

### *Experienced Mothers and Extremely Fussy Babies*

Experienced mothers with two or three previous children may also experience an extremely fussy baby.

### "A Joy to All of Us"

"Before, Michael would scream and cry for hours and nothing we did seemed to help him. We would rock him, walk with him and he would still scream. He even fought the bottle. This would go on for four or five hours straight; then he'd fall asleep and sleep for approximately an hour then start all over again. We didn't know what to do to pacify him because nothing seemed to help, and we felt sorry for him because we hated to see our son like that and not be able to help him. Once Michael started sitting up, it relieved him somewhat and now he is a very happy and content baby boy. He smiles, goos and coos and is starting to sleep more, and it seems to be a peaceful sleep. When he is awake now he is content and doesn't have to be held, rocked or walked constantly. He is a joy to all of us."

### "Tremendous Difference"

"David seems to be very content in whatever we do with him; he also is very content on where we lay him down, observes everything quietly and amuses himself by watching the mobile in his crib. He also accepts changes in his routine very well. It's a tremendous difference from when he had extreme fussiness."

Perhaps you will recognize in these descriptions of children during and after extreme fussiness ends some of the things that your child is going through. Be comforted. This is all very typical. As these testimonials show, even the fussiest children outgrow extreme fussiness and become sweeter. Some turn into dream babies; others continue to be more assertive, but all become much more responsive, predictable, and easy to live with.

Labeling your child's fussiness/crying as 'extreme fussiness/colic' tends to emphasize her worst behavior. Her good behavior is just as much a part of her personality. Closely observe your baby at her best, her worst, and when awake and when asleep. Treasure the beautiful, smiling moments. This is your preview of the baby you may be living with soon.

# III

## HOW SOOTHING YOUR NEWBORN MAKES A SWEET BABY

# 11

## After Extreme Fussiness Ends: No Sleep Problems

*Nature Conditions Nurture*

Your newborn's fussiness compels you to put forth more effort to soothe.

*Nurture Becomes Nature*

Your extra effort to soothe your newborn will create a sweet baby.

There is, as we have seen a significant connection between extreme fussiness and later sleep problems. Not all extremely fussy babies become poor sleepers, though, and not all babies with sleep problems went through a period of extreme fussiness. So let's look at infant sleep disorders in a more general way.

*What Is A Good Night's Sleep?*

We do not know what sleep is for. That is, we do not understand the biological function of sleep. Some say that sleep evolved to prevent our prehistoric ancestors from hurting themselves bumping around in the dark!

The restorative power of sleep is a medical mystery. Ideally, sleep makes us feel at peace with ourselves and the world. However, some adults that were observed in a sleep laboratory said that they did not feel restored or rested even after appearing to sleep well. When their brain wave activity was analyzed, it sometimes appeared distorted. Apparently the **quality** of sleep is as important as the **quantity**. The brain is not simply a chemical battery that is recharged by sleep.

We cannot ask babies if they have had a good night's sleep. We know about qualitative differences in newborns sleep patterns but we can't say what exactly are the elements of sleep that constitute 'good' quality sleep. We do know that tired parents, kept awake because their crybaby is screaming, cannot easily function as loving mothers and fathers. A sleeping problem for your baby means a sleeping problem for you. You will be encouraged to know that many infant sleep disorders can be modified.

### *Does Your Baby Have a Sleep Problem?*

Sometimes it is hard to tell if there is a sleep problem. Most mothers do not mind getting up a few times at night to feed their babies during the first few weeks. Typically, these babies awaken once or twice and immediately fall asleep after a 10 to 15 minute feeding. By several weeks many babies awaken only once. Consider yourself fortunate if your baby sleeps this well. Not all infants do.

One mother of an extremely fussy infant told me that she had fantasies of having just one night of uninterrupted sleep. She could not remember, she said, when she last felt rested. In the playground, when other mothers talked about their babies rolling over or sitting up, she talked only about her baby not sleeping. She wanted to attack those mothers whose children slept through the night; what had they done to deserve such luck? Her baby was several months old and still got up frequently every night and seemed never to want to sleep.

There was a sharp edge of desperation in the mother's request for help. She was almost out of patience waiting for the baby to outgrow this problem. We discussed how sleep patterns relate to awake behaviors, and how her baby had developed her sleep problem. After an extended explanation she knew what the problem was and how to solve it. This chapter will give you that explanation and treatment plan for your baby's sleeping problem.

### *What's Enough Sleep for a Newborn?*

Sleep patterns in the newborn and during the first few months of life develop in a predictable fashion. During the first few days of life, there does not seem to be much individual stability regarding the duration of sleep time. That is, some babies change from being good sleepers to bad sleepers and back again. However, between six and thirty-three months of age, the total sleep duration, and longest sleep period usually were observed to be stable individual characteristics. Individual infants who are brief duration sleepers tend to remain that way. In this respect, sleep duration is like crying behavior and temperament—it shows little consistency at first, but after a few months it develops into a moderately stable individual characteristic. There are no significant sleep duration differences between boys and girls.

### *What Determines How Much a Baby Sleeps?*

The emergence of sleep patterns in the first few months is due to changes in the brain as it matures. Most of these changes occur in an orderly and predictable fashion. For example, as you get older, the duration of sleep decreases. In babies, there is a dramatic shift in the pattern of sleep states at three to four months.

The three- or four-month birthday appears to be an important milestone for sleep development. After this point, infants' sleep patterns tend to resemble those of adults. The normal adult cycling from quiet non-REM sleep to active REM sleep, emerges at about four months of age and stays that way for the rest of an individual's life.

Contrary to popular belief, sleep duration is not influenced by introducing solid foods. Slipping a little cereal into that nighttime bottle will not really help. This fact has been documented in several studies where parents kept careful daily records of feeding and sleeping patterns. In France, there was a study of a group of infants who were never hungry. Because of birth defects involving their intestine or stomach, these infants were fed continuously through their veins. Even when their hunger rhythms were suppressed, the sleep-wake patterns remained unchanged. There were partial awakenings, called arousals or light sleep stages just as occur in healthy babies. In other words, older infants partially or completely wake up because sometimes their brain, not their stomach, turns on an alarm clock. Of course the infant will drink or nurse if offered the opportunity, but this is probably only to encourage the parent to stay a little longer. Frequent non-nutritive or recreational snacking in the middle of the night is a form of social interaction that soothes the baby back to sleep, but older infants learn quickly that if they don't suck when offered the opportunity, even if not hungry, then their mother or father will more quickly put them down and leave. Of course, sometimes a baby is hungry and awakens to be fed.

Do breast-fed babies awaken more often than bottle-fed babies? Two studies on this subject, one of which was mine, reached opposite conclusions. However, there is no doubt that switching from breast to bottle or giving a supplemental bottle at night does not help babies consistently sleep through the night.

### Night Wakings Are Normal

Awakenings at night are common in healthy infants, perhaps more common than their parents realize. Videotaping of infants at home has shown that they often awaken and return to sleep without calling out or crying. Brief episodes of night waking may reflect the biological sleep rhythms occurring at night. We know that during the non-REM state, sleep alternates between deep sleep and light sleep. In some children, the "light" stage is probably so light that they awaken partially or completely. This is not a problem unless it regularly disturbs the parents or keeps the child from getting enough sleep. As he grows, a child should develop his own resources to return to sleep without his parents' help.

In one study of over one hundred infants, researchers focused on awakenings accompanied by crying or fussing between midnight and 5:00 A.M. which occurred at least once a week. By age three months, 70 percent of the babies had no night awakenings. By age six months, 83 percent of all babies were sleeping through the night, and by one year of age 90 percent of babies slept through the night. Again it should be noted that settling, or no night waking, was not related to the sex of the baby, birth weight, or weight at age three months. Also, the mother's personality did not appear to influence night waking.

### Boy-Girl Differences

A study of night waking using home videotape measurements observed that male infants had more irregular sleep schedules than females. Our study at the Children's Memorial Hospital also showed that parents perceived night waking to be a problem in their sons more often than in their daughters; even though daughters awoke as often as sons! Therefore, the perception of night waking as a problem—unlike extreme fussiness or difficult temperament problems—might be a bit sex-specific.

### Parental Response

Infants who cry more and infants who slept less over 24 hours tend to have more night wakings than infants who cry less and sleep longer. In one study, the mothers' behavior toward the night waking was divided into three patterns: always feeding, never feeding, and sometimes feeding. The group of babies who were fed "sometimes" described in the study as receiving **inconsistent handling**, had significantly more awakenings.

It seems that inconsistent parental responses to night waking in older infants may encourage the habit, magnify the problem, and lead to more crying at night and more difficulties in the infant returning to sleep. This pattern is referred to as "trained night crying," and may be a common sequel to extreme fussiness behavior.

### When Older Babies Wake at Night

Interestingly, about half of all infants who settled before five months of age will begin night waking between six and twelve months. Many mothers have asked me, "What am I doing wrong? Why is he getting me up now after sleeping through the night these past months?" Perhaps the baby is now more curious and attentive to his surroundings. Another explanation is that at about four months of age, the baby's bedtime drifts earlier, towards 6-8 P.M. By respecting you baby's need for an earlier bedtime, we don't force this on him, it is natural to feed him earlier. Thus, don't be surprised if between four and nine months of age, your child now is awakening once or twice for a feeding.

Night waking is a very common problem in older babies. Up to 40 percent of mothers describe problems in putting their child to sleep or problems in having him sleep through the night. If your child has a sleeping problem, you are not alone.

I advise mothers of older babies to be consistent in their response to night waking. During the first few months, always respond promptly to your baby's crying. After four, five, certainly six months, it is time to change your tactics. Begin by trying to analyze whether there is any special reason for your baby waking at night.

*Why Older Infants Awaken*

## 1. The Wrong Sleep Schedule

Frequent night awakening sometimes seems to stem from an inappropriate sleep schedule. As you know, the body has its own internal rhythms, which ideally are in internal synchrony with deep sleep, light sleep, and wakefulness and collectively in synchrony with external light dark cycles.

An imposed sleep schedule that is out of sync with the child's biological rhythms (such as body temperature, hormone secretion, etc.) might distort sleep patterns. Healthy, restorative sleep depends on **timing** the evening sleep onsets and morning awakenings, so that they can occur when the body's temperature and endocrine levels are right. Sleep scheduling, or the **timing** of when sleep take place is as important as sleep **duration**.

Do not become enchanted by claims that babies simply fall asleep whenever they are tired, regardless of circumstances. Yes, there are infants who can nap in the stroller, at a party, in the car. But most of these are exhausted infants who have collapsed. Most infants never adapt to this kind of behavior. They do not rest well unless it is dark and quiet. Protect your baby's natural sleeping schedule. Do not try to force the baby to adjust her sleeping patterns to your lifestyle.

## 2. Parental Reinforcement

Parents often unintentionally contribute to their child's bad sleep habits. This is particularly true when the baby has been extremely fussy and the parents have gotten used to rocking and walking with him. When the child continues to want this attention at night, the parents don't realize they are reinforcing a bad habit. Often they are on "automatic pilot": it is 3:00 A.M., they are half-asleep and all they know is that they must promptly attend to the baby or the crying will surely get worse.

The same thing might happen during the day. Older infants who awaken frequently at night also take abnormally brief naps. The baby loses sleep and the mother misses an opportunity to catch up on her own rest. Often these babies would learn to take longer naps if they were not picked up from their cribs at the first whimper.

### 3. Your Cranky Baby May Just Be Tired

Some parents, especially parents whose children have been extremely fussy, seem unable to tell when their babies are simply exhausted. Mothers often tell me that their infants do not need as much sleep as other infants. They report, no doubt accurately, that their babies never rub their eyes, yawn, put their heads down, or appear to be tired. These mothers don't realize that short-tempered, irritable, hyperactive behavior is also a sign of fatigue. Some mothers use the fact that their child occasionally falls asleep in stores, parks, or other noisy places as "proof" that the child has no sleep problem. On the contrary, this could mean that the infant has become so totally exhausted that he simply conks out.

Sleep deprivation affects mood much more than it does activity. We see this in adults who as part of an experiment reduce their nightly sleep duration. They were usually able to function well the next day. As long as they get about five hours of sleep a night, they can complete tasks, show adaptive physical skills, and appear to be quite capable of thinking through problems. But they feel awful. They report feeling slightly or very ill. Their temperament changes radically. So imagine the effect of insufficient sleep on a young child.

A good way to tell whether your child is getting enough sleep is to observe how he behaves when awakening. Babies who are sleeping enough are pleasant and playful; babies who never get enough rest awaken crying and grimacing and

omfortable for no apparent reason. Re-
', overactive behavior is as clear an indica-
tion of fatigue as is yawning or dozing off. It is not true that
infants simply doze off whenever they are tired. Many need
help in getting themselves to sleep.

### Treatment of Trained Night Crying

### 1. Let the Baby Alone

The best way to manage trained night crying in an infant
over four or five months of age is to feed him only once or
twice and at all other times to consistently leave him alone at
night, even if he cries. This always works if, and only if, the
bedtime is reasonably early and naps are in place. Within a
few days you will see a reduction in the frequency and duration of nighttime crying spells. Before long your baby will
learn to sleep through the night.

### 2. Learn to Be Consistent

Consistency is the key to breaking this habit. Parents who
have been through the ups and down and twists and turns of
extreme fussiness may find this a big change. For as long as
you have known this baby, you have had to be flexible; now
you must make an about-face and be consistent. Please believe that your baby is ready for a routine, even if he has
never been in the past. Realize that you have a few habits of
your own to change: you will have to stop letting the baby
"call the tune." You will now set the schedule, and let the
baby cry until he sleeps. You will have to harden your heart
a tiny bit, after months of flooding your baby with sympathy and prompt attention. Once you and he make the transition your life will be easier and more predictable and, believe
me, your baby will be happier too. But you are going to have
to teach yourselves a new pattern of parenting.

### 3. Reduce External Stimulation

For the child who had extreme fussiness and/or is very stimulus sensitive, then reducing the amount of external stimulation might help your baby sleep.

Begin by modifying the child's bedroom. To get the room completely dark, mount opaque blackout shades on the outer molding of the window and hold them in place with curtains, tape, or picture framing. Obviously, there should be no night-light and the door should be almost completely closed. If you need to cool the room with a window air-conditioner, run it before the infant goes to bed and turn it off when he sleeps. Keep the windows closed to eliminate street noises. You might cover central air ducts to reduce the clicking on and off noises of the heating or air conditioning system. A steady background noise from a vaporizer, humidifier, or "white noise" machine might help drown out intermittent sounds. Of course, you should not run the garbage disposal, dishwasher, or vacuum cleaner during naptime. If possible, turn the telephone off; turn on your answering machine. Do not go into the child's room or even open his door to peek in.

Crib toys and accessories should be removed except for one special security blanket or doll. The bedroom is a place to sleep; it is not a playground.

Making your child's room pitch dark and quiet should be thought of as only a temporary measure. You will not make your child permanently dependent upon these conditions in order to sleep. In the future, you will be able to have dinner parties and go on vacations and your child will sleep. A remarkable change occurs when your baby sleeps well for several weeks or months in a peaceful environment. Gradually, the child appears less jumpy, less irritable, less restless, and more able to attend to one thing at a time. This overall decreased behavioral responsiveness suggests a decrease in the state of arousal, which probably results from the change to better-quality sleep or sleep that is uninterrupted and prolonged. Now that the child is better rested, he is less likely to fight going to sleep and he is less likely to be thoroughly awakened when the telephone rings or the garage door opens. He still may be a light sleeper, compared to other children, but he won't behave as if his nervous system was always excitable.

## Begin with Bedtime

Maintain a regular sleep schedule, with bedtime and wake-up time at the same hours every day. Establish night-time rituals and stick to them. Fathers should be involved in these rituals and should sometimes place the child in bed after the mother has nursed. Read a book or sing the same medley of songs every night. Make bedtime a happy time; do not act as though you expect a struggle, do not make going to bed seem like a punishment. The earlier the bed time, the better in order to avoid the over-tired state.

Children will learn to fall asleep (or fall back asleep if they wake later) because it is dark, quiet, and boring in the bedroom alone. Once you start leaving the child alone at night, do not relent. The goal is to teach her that she will get no further companionship from you until morning.

### Parents: No Excuses!

It is difficult to say that it is all right to leave a baby alone and let her cry. Sometimes a father who is the only wage earner demands that the mother quiet the child so that he can get his rest. Mothers also worry about disturbing other people: children, resident in-laws, or neighbors.

Sometimes parents are afraid of hurting their baby's feelings or making him angry. They are supported in this fear by a number of popular infant-care books which say that leaving a child to cry will make him feel abandoned, give him a complex, and cause him to resent you forever. In my opinion, it is absurd to believe that a few hours of crying will undo the thousands of hours of love, tenderness, and security that you give your baby. Children are very resilient; their psyches are tough, they appear to forget quickly, and they do not carry grudges. You will find, I guarantee, that even when it has taken your little guy hours to cry himself to sleep, he will be cheerful, affectionate, and glad to see you in the morning. Anyway, this may be the first time but certainly will not be the last time in your child's life that you will have to do something for his good health which might seem to make him unhappy at the time.

Prolonged uninterrupted sleep that is occurring on the right schedule is a health habit. You can teach sleep hygiene just as you would teach other important health habits such as hand washing, regular exercise, teeth brushing, good nutrition, buckle-up in cars, wear helmets when on bikes, and sun safety.

Occasionally parents have hidden conflicts that get in the way of their resolve. Perhaps a career woman simultaneously wants to stay at home and nurse her baby but also wants to return to work. Depending on how she is feeling at any given time, she may leave the child alone or she may rush to his side. This inconsistent behavior encourages the night awakening and crying.

Some mothers cannot let their child cry because they imagine some illness is causing the night awakening. They may exaggerate minor common colds or rashes. One family decided that their fourteen-month-old child was awakening early every morning because of a gastrointestinal problem. Undigested vegetable matter in the child's stools "proved" this. I examined the stools, reassured the mother that many healthy children have frequent loose stools, and told her that these same children often have sleep problems. When the family realized that the child would outgrow this chronic, nonspecific diarrhea and that it did not mean he had a disease, they focused their efforts on behaviorally managing the sleep problem by letting the child get himself back to sleep.

Another family blamed all nighttime problems on teething. From the age of six months on, the child was imagined to be constantly suffering from some painful tooth eruption. But, surprise! Letting this baby cry at night cured the teething pain for good.

### Make the Decision

Helping your child break a bad sleep habit is a major task. Fortunately, it is quickly accomplished, but it will be hard on you. It might be worth waiting until the parents can take time off from work. You may be up all night or get only fragments of sleep, and working during this time could be difficult, if not dangerous.

Be sure to discuss your plans with your other children. Explain to them that the baby will be crying at night because you are breaking a bad habit. Make sure your older children know that you are not punishing the baby and that he's not suffering.

Warn your neighbors if they are within earshot. Explain that the treatment will last only a few nights and will put an end to the nighttime crying which has probably been bothering them, too.

### And Then Do It

Don't be surprised when your baby cries for a long time with great gusto the first couple of nights. She wants a return of the old style of parental attention and will put forth extra energy to that end. Remember that your baby will not hurt her lungs or vocal cords, choke, suffocate, or anything else. Do not become alarmed. Do not weaken. Do not peek into the bedroom; this will only recharge your baby's battery.

During a few days of sleep training, there will be more crying per day than ever before. But, and this is a very important point, if you allow an over-tired state to develop and persist, there will be much more total crying spread out over months or years. Parents naturally tend to worry too much about the possible harmful effects of a few days of crying and fail to see the long term damaging effects of a stressed

family living with a chronically over-tired child, then tod-
dler, then adolescent.

When your baby cries and cries the first night the mother
should wear earplugs, take long showers, go to the basement
or got for a walk. Dear mothers, get away from the crying! It
will tear at your heart. Let your husband sit outside the door
of the infant's room. Use your ingenuity: one family lived in
a small house with no place to escape from the baby's crying.
The father borrowed a friend's camper-van and parked it in
the driveway at night. On alternate nights the parents took
turns sleeping in the van so that one parent was always
rested. Another family found that only if both parents stayed
together could they give each other the strength to resist the
temptation to rush to the baby's side. Do what works for
you.

The typical sequence is for the baby to cry for several
hours the first night, and to awaken frequently throughout
the night. Sometimes the second night is worse as your baby
tries even harder to get back to the old pattern of enjoying
the company of parents at night. Or during the second night
there might be a briefer initial crying period and fewer,
briefer night awakenings. The parents usually note that the
morning after the second night the child awakens later than
usual. He is probably tired from two nights of strenuous crying. By the third night, there is substantially less crying.
Many parents report that for the first time the child appears
tired around the bedtime hour. Usually there are few to no
awakenings by the fourth or fifth night.

### If It Doesn't Work

If you let your baby cry according to these suggestions and you see no improvement after a few days, perhaps
the child is too young. I have seen this plan fail (though
rarely) in babies five and six months of age. However, by
eight or nine months, when the parents try it again, it always
works. I believe this four-day treatment is worth trying every
three or four weeks from six months of age on.

*Improvement*

When the parents succeed in encouraging regular sleep habits, the child becomes much easier to live with. The increased rest for both child and parents makes a world of difference.

After several months without night awakenings, the parents can relax the strict routine somewhat. They can take trips with the child, cope with an illness (such as an ear infection) which interrupts sleep, and be less rigid in maintaining the sleep schedule when social activities occur. Once the special event or ear infection is over, the parents should resume their consistent regular handling and the child will again start sleeping through the night.

*Drugs to Make Your Baby Sleep*

I have saved discussion of sedative drugs for last because I do not believe they can solve behavioral problems. It has been my experience that parents view drugs as a quick fix and make no effort to change their behavior. Therefore, despite a few days of improvement, the problems continue. I don't think drugs play any role in the management of trained night crying. One popular book emphasizes unrestricted breast-feeding and the family bed as the solution to all sleep problems, but then the author states that if problems still occur, use chloral hydrate to knock out the baby! This is wrong and only reflects on the authors misunderstanding of what sleep is all about. No melatonin, no progesterone, no tryptophan, no drugs.

*Not All Night Waking Is a Problem*

I want to emphasize that this approach—letting the baby cry as long as necessary—is appropriate only in the case of trained night crying. If your baby awakens at night only occasionally, if his fussiness comes from a verified fever or ear infection pain, if he seems to need comfort when there has been a change in his life—then, by all means, comfort him. He will not develop a bad habit if you go to him a few nights out of the month. Just be sure you are not using teething or "what happened during the day" as an excuse night after night. As Dr. Illingworth, the dean of infant crying research, wrote: "No baby should ever be left crying for prolonged periods—except when one is breaking a habit produced by mismanagement."

# 12

## How We Taught Our Baby to Sleep

*Some Mothers Talk About Their Experiences*

The cycle of exhaustion, fussiness, poor sleep habits, and sleep deprivation is a baffling one to families in the midst of it. On the surface, nothing seems terribly amiss, yet everything is wrong. Baby and parents reinforce each other's bizarre schedules. Other problems are blamed. Where there once was extreme fussiness, parents assume it mutated into new and equally distressing forms.

Following are accounts by some of the mothers who have consulted me for their children's sleep problems. All of these babies once had extreme fussiness. I have quoted at length in order to convey the relentless, unpredictable nature of trained night crying. Some of these stories are bound to make any mother feel lucky by comparison. While they show how a sleep problem can get out of hand, and how it can masquerade as something else; they also show how easily it can be corrected once it is identified.

Here is a thirty-two-year-old mother with professional training. You'll notice that despite the professionals she consulted and all of the approaches she tried, no one addressed the issue of sleep, the most obvious problem.

### Joel's Mother

"Looking back, my concern for Joel started in the hospital: the nurses said that he cried all the time in the nursery and would bring him to me for feeding and comforting—often at hourly intervals. I left the hospital exhausted. Since Joel is my only child, and I am an only child, I had little to compare him with. The first three months home were brutal and, although I suspected as much, I didn't admit until he was almost four months old, that his behavior wasn't normal.' I guess that is something no parent ever wants to see—or believe.

"Life with Joel during those months was disruptive and draining. He had no schedule, slept very little (maybe eight hours in a twenty-four-hour period, in one- to three-hour blocks) and cried a good deal of the time. Meeting Joel's needs filled my day; besides feeding him and changing him, the major task was keeping him quiet. Several things worked at different times; walking him in his infant seat, especially outside, while singing; car rides; visiting anywhere; carriage rides. We became vagabonds. Often a day would include several carriage rides, some lasting up to ninety minutes; a trip to the store; and a visit with a friend. After only five hours of interrupted sleep each night, I found it hard to get back to sleep. I'd be exhausted. But I couldn't stop moving.

"Bedtime for Joel was usually 10:00 P.M. We couldn't just put him in his crib. I had to rock him, walk him, nurse him, and lay him down ever so gently. He would usually wake up once during the process and we'd have to begin again. The process in total generally took an hour. I'd then fall into bed hoping I could unwind and get to sleep quickly, knowing that I'd be up two to three times that night and up for good at 5:00 to 5:30 A.M.

"I waited as patiently as I could for Joel to get his act together. I'd heard that at three to four months extremely fussy babies miraculously became settled and slept through the night. At three months Joel did sleep through the night for approximately six days. A start, we thought, but it quickly ended.

"By Joel's four-month checkup, I was completely demoralized. I prayed he had an ear infection to explain his irritability and lack of sleep. When he was given a clean bill of health, I cried. The pediatrician suggested a sedative. When I filled the prescription the pharmacist told me that the medication was an antihistamine, one sometimes used to make a fussy baby go to sleep.

"I decided then to get a second opinion. Joel could get to sleep—he needed help staying asleep. I put the medication aside and headed for the telephone. Although I felt physically drained myself—hanging on by my fingertips, having to go on despite my physical exhaustion—my greatest anxiety was reserved for Joel. I wanted to help him. He was in discomfort and the world must have seemed a terrible place to him. I felt so responsible, yet unable to reckon with what I needed to do, and no one to tell me. He wasn't an extremely fussy baby any more, but he cried a lot and couldn't be comforted. It was obvious that he wanted to sleep, but couldn't. I felt so helpless.

"The new pediatrician was supportive but gave few answers. Joel seemed healthy. We did detect a hip problem—though nothing painful enough to explain the poor sleeping pattern.

"During this time, I also contacted the local Birth to Three program for help. The child development specialist there felt that Joel was hypersensitive and irritable, lacked bilateral integration, and showed an uncharacteristic-for-his-age, strong preference for his right side. She agreed that Joel was different from other babies and might need a different approach. She gave recommendations for dealing with the motor delays, but seemed cool to the idea of letting Joel cry. Joel also saw a physical therapist from Birth to Three whom confirmed what the child development specialist saw. He suggested that the cause' could be just a developmental delay, a nervous system that wasn't quite ready to stabilize, or a mild brain injury that might or might not repair itself with time.

"Now I was busy with exercises for Joel's hip that the physical therapist recommended as well as other activities suggested by the Birth to Three specialists to help improve Joel's left side functioning and bilateral integration.

"No one addressed the issue of sleep. By the time Joel was eight months old, his irritability had decreased some but his sleep patterns had not improved. On the days he was rested, he was charming. In fact, even when he wasn't rested he could appear jovial and content—as long as we kept moving. At this time I issued an edict: no more night feeding. I'd feed Joel at 9:30 P.M., his bedtime, and at 5:00 A.M., his waking time, but not in between. I felt he was ready for this.

"My husband became Joel's 'walker.' Once to twice a night, he'd go to Joel and walk him back to sleep. The first few months of Joel's life had been mine, these next few were his father's. In the early months, it was 'Joel must be hungry,' or 'I have to go to work,' so Mother dealt with Joel. Now Mother bowed out and Dad finally began to believe that maybe something really was wrong with Joel. Mother didn't actually sleep more, but at least I spent more time in bed!

"Our marriage was really strained during Joel's first year. We couldn't take out our frustrations on Joel, so we took them out on each other. Looking back, some of my behavior was hysterical and irrational. My husband seemed to do a lot of denying. We both realized our behavior was related to physical exhaustion, but we seemed unable to reverse the direction.

"I saw an announcement in a local paper about an infant sleep disorders center. They sent me a questionnaire; I filled it out immediately. The questions make me think perhaps there were other children like Joel.

"At the center Dr. Weissbluth agreed that Joel was healthy. Joel, he said, just needed some sleep, and so did his parents. The fact that the doctor had seen other children like Joel, and that they had improved, was reassuring. The doctor's confidence in his procedure was encouraging, but did he really know Joel? I was hooked by the doctor's promise to follow up by phone to check Joel's progress during the course of the treatment to get Joel to sleep. I could scream at him if it didn't work and he could share the frustration.

"Something inside told me that at nine and one half months Joel was ready and I was ready too for his development. I liked the doctor's picture of my assuming a parenting role with Joel—not letting him cry 'but teaching him to sleep,' letting him become independent and learning to get to sleep on his own.

"Anyway, we all were ready. And, with a few setbacks, it worked in two days. I believe it worked because Joel's system had matured. Could it have worked sooner? Joel was nine and one half months old. Maybe he was ready a month earlier, but earlier than that, I'm not sure.

"It helped us not only to be given permission to let Joel get himself to sleep in his own crib, but in fact to be told it was a parental responsibility. With a baby who slept through the night and napped twice a day, our lives not so much improved as began again. I feel we're normal now."

This distressing sequence of events is not uncommon. Nor is it uncommon that the mother tried everything, took all advice, drove herself frantic, even believed for a time that her son had a brain injury, when all they needed was sleep.

Another mother, a twenty-seven-year-old homemaker with a partial college education, described her experiences ("our ten-month ordeal") with her first daughter as follows:

### Melissa's Mother

"My husband, Kevin, and I were blessed with a beautiful baby girl on June 13, 1981. We were so happy, but it was definitely a change in the household. I started breastfeeding and I wasn't very successful, so after two weeks Melissa was put on formula. I really don't think it was easy for Melissa to settle in. Two weeks after she was born we moved from an apartment into a house. It was a really chaotic time for all of us.

"After a month or so in the house we all felt better being settled in, but we became sure of one thing—Melissa had extreme fussiness. She was not on any kind of schedule and the most she slept was about four hours at one time. This was not always consistent either. At this time we didn't consider her not sleeping too much of a problem. Being new parents, we weren't exactly sure how things were supposed to be or what we should do.

"After the extreme fussiness stage was supposed to have ended we started worrying because Melissa still was not sleeping. Consulting her pediatrician on many occasions, we tried everything: different formulas, Donnatal, chamomile tea, warm clothes on her tummy, Tylenol. We even tried the Rail Runner, a train put on the rail of her crib that played music and moved back and forth very slowly. Within fifteen minutes Melissa was supposed to be sound asleep. No luck.

"For ten months, nothing we did worked. During this time everyone had advice to give us. Some of the comments were: Maybe you just have a baby that won't sleep. 'You are spoiling her by holding her all the time so she will sleep.' 'Just leave her in the crib and let her scream.' 'When she's ready she'll fall into a schedule.' I was so confused! Kevin and I would talk about the situation and our worry was that something was wrong with Melissa, even though she appeared to be a totally healthy baby.

"We loved her so much that we worked our schedules around Melissa. We both were like walking zombies. I would hold Melissa and give her a bottle so she might get an hour or two of sleep. As soon as I laid her in the crib she would start crying. At times I was so tired I would lay her next to me on our bed and pray for one hour of sleep. I would spend all day in my pajamas tending to Melissa. Since Kevin's sleep was more important due to a full-time job, I would sleep when he got home from work for two to three hours and the rest of the time I would catnap when Melissa did. The longest period of time I was up without sleep was seventy-two hours. I had to call Kevin home from work because I couldn't stand up anymore.

"It was a physically and emotionally trying time for Kevin and myself. We argued a lot and we really weren't communicating with each other. We were both just too tired to even talk sometimes. We didn't have much of a love life, but it was our strong love for each other that held all three of us together. I would cry a lot and pray that soon Melissa would sleep.

"Melissa was so happy and good under the circumstances. I would look at her while she was awake and be amazed. How can she be so playful and alert? She's not getting enough sleep!' She even had dark circles under her eyes.

"Well, after ten months Kevin saw an excerpt on the news about sleep problems in children. We decided to get more information. I called and we were sent a questionnaire to fill out. Kevin and I felt this was our last hope.

"We talked with Dr. Weissbluth about Melissa and he checked her over. After our discussion he said that we had to put Melissa on a regular schedule. Even if she cried we had to leave her in the crib during naps and nighttime. We could use music and a fan, but had to make sure almost everything was out of her crib and the room was dark. He told us this procedure should show results in about seven days. I remember crying all the way home but Kevin reassured me that it was for Melissa's own good as well as ours.

"We started on a Friday night. Kevin stayed with Melissa and I went to stay at my mom's. I knew if I stayed home I would be in tears all the time and we probably wouldn't have gone through with it.

"It wasn't as bad as I had imagined. Kevin told me that Melissa cried for about forty-five minutes and then fell asleep. She also got up in the night and cried, but not for very long. He left her in the crib no matter what.

"After the first night she adapted very well. It was harder trying to get her to take a nap, but after about two to three weeks on constant reinforcement we had a baby who enjoyed sleeping. We would put her down for the night at 7:30 P.M., and she would sleep until 7:00 A.M. the next morning. Her naps would range from two to four hours, one nap a day. Believe me, we had a lot to celebrate on Melissa's first birthday!

"Now Melissa is sixteen months old. She cries in her sleep

from time to time, due to teething or illness, but at least we know what is wrong and we can help her. We have a beautiful daughter whom we love very much. Kevin and I can now enjoy a good night's sleep and peace of mind."

Another sensitive, intelligent thirty-eight-year-old mother went through a seventeen-month-long series of explanations for her son's problem before discovering it was a sleep disturbance. As you will see, she blamed hunger, the food she was eating, the medicine she was taking, the makeup she was wearing, flu, hyperactivity, teething, Tylenol, etc. Time and again she believed she had solved the problem, only to have it recur. Let me assure you, as the doctor who examined David, that despite the mother's harrowing descriptions of bloody stools, throwing up, bulging eyes, etc., there was never anything physically wrong with David. Please consider reading this account twice, first paying attention to how the baby behaved, and then focusing on how the mother behaved.

### David's Mother

"David is seventeen months old and for the first time I can honestly say I enjoy him and being a mother. With him sleeping through the night, I see a tremendous personality change. He has suddenly come alive and has taken a greater interest in his environment. He explores the outside rather than asking to be carried. He is no longer terrified of new situations and is beginning to interact with other children. He actually sits down and plays with his toys. Most important, he is now a happy, affectionate baby.

"I feel a very large load has been taken off me. I know now it was David's extreme fussiness and lack of sleep that affected his behavior, not my mothering. Up until now, no matter how I tried to convince myself otherwise, I was certain it was my fault.

"Why? Our first pediatrician considered David to be a 'well baby.' He was the type of doctor who believed a baby wasn't ill unless he had a terrible disease like cystic fibrosis. He never even suggested we might have a baby with extreme fussiness. Through the first five miserable months, he repeatedly told us there was nothing wrong with David; he was gaining weight, therefore he was healthy.

"All I had to do was compare David with other babies his age and I knew there was something wrong. I assumed that it had to be my mothering. He was not comfortable enough to sleep during the day, sit in an infant seat or ride in a buggy without crying. He was up three times a night, each time for at least forty-five minutes. Whenever he was up he wanted to be held.

"He was so hungry that, initially, he rejected nursing. It took too long and he found it too difficult to suck. I remember feeling personally rejected when he refused to nurse, but I wanted to badly and continued to try. It took three weeks to get him to nurse without giving him a short drink from the bottle first. During that time he would scream before a feeding, drink for a short period, then scream again and double up with stomach cramps. I hung on, hoping the nursing would get better.

"The only information I had about nursing and a mother's diet during nursing was from books. Our pediatrician never offered any information or reasons for my child's behavior.

"When David was one month old, the flu bouts started. I began to have flu-like symptoms, diarrhea and severe cramps. The next day David would begin throwing up, having diarrhea with mucus and severe cramps. My flu lasted a few days each episode; his lasted exactly ten days. This occurred five different times before his three-month checkup. Each time, we called the pediatrician and he reassured us. As long as David wasn't dehydrated and had gained weight at his last checkup, the doctor said we shouldn't worry.

"I finally realized every time I ate chop suey, it seemed to make both of us sick. I had never reacted to Chinese food before but it seemed like the pregnancy and delivery changed my system. The MSG must have had a violent effect on both of us!

"During this time, I was becoming increasingly depressed. I was making my baby sick and feeling incredibly guilty

about it. Many well-meaning friends and relatives urged me
to stop nursing. I was hearing terrific comments like 'There
must be something wrong with your milk,' or 'What have
you been eating to make David sick again?'

"After David's three-month checkup, he began having
screaming bouts that were so severe his eyes bulged. There
was no way to comfort him. Also during this time, David's
stools changed to dark green with mucus and traces of
blood.

"Bill and I were very worried. We were tired of the plati-
tudes from our pediatrician. When we pushed him for more
help he suggested we take David in for an upper and lower
G.I.

"It was obviously time to find a new doctor. A friend referred Dr. K. In my first telephone conversation with the
new doctor, he asked me more questions than my first pediatrician did during the entire time he was treating David.

"We focused on my diet. I eliminated milk products and
slowly stopped those foods I was eating on a daily basis that
might affect David. Nothing seemed to help.

"Then the pediatrician questioned me about medication I
might be using. I was taking an antihistamine for allergies.
He suggested I stop for a few days because of the yellow dye.
I seemed to have a new baby. His stools changed from green
to yellow. He stopped screaming. He was calmer and happier. We were ecstatic. I very much wanted to believe everything would be fine.

"I started a new antihistamine with a green dye. David reacted again, but this time worse than ever. I tried several
white allergy medications until I found one that didn't make
either one of us sick.

"At this point, my pediatrician suggested we read a book
on hyperactive children. We didn't want to read it, but then
David had a reaction to the dyes in children's Tylenol.

"When he was six months old, we gave him Tylenol for
what we thought was teething pain. The pain got worse and
we gave him more Tylenol. This continued until I realized his
reactions were too severe to be teeth related. I couldn't hold

him. He never stopped moving. He'd crawl down my leg, continuously squirm in my arms, bang his head against objects, and grab at our faces and scream. As bad as his sleeping was before, it was now much worse. There were some nights when he was up for hours either staring into space or constantly moving.

"Bill and I read Feingold and were convinced he was writing about our baby. We tried to reassure ourselves that David wasn't seriously ill, but in our guts I don't think it really helped. Our kid was hyperactive. We were in too much pain to question the book or ask for another opinion.

"Since David was nursing exclusively, I went on the Feingold diet and eliminated foods with dyes and chemicals in them. Just to play safe, I also eliminated milk and egg products in case David was allergic to them. There were days he seemed improved but would then have another reaction. I would play detective and frantically search for the cause of his reactions. I even stopped using toothpaste and wearing lipstick.

"When David was seven months old, I couldn't stand nursing anymore. I was convinced I was poisoning my baby. I hired a nurse for a week to relieve me and to help me wean him. David screamed for ten hours straight while the nurse held him and offered him a bottle. He wouldn't even close his mouth on the nipple. Bill became concerned that the weaning by a stranger was traumatic for David and he wanted it stopped. By that time, I couldn't listen to the baby scream anymore. So I continued to nurse.

"Shortly after we tried to wean, Bill went out of the country for ten days. I was in terrible shape. It was bad enough trying to cope with David with Bill's help, but alone it seemed impossible. Because I was in such bad shape emotionally, Dr. K suggested I wean him cold turkey; that is, we'd leave David with a nurse for the weekend and he'd be weaned when we returned.

"I must have been a wreck to even consider it. When Bill came home, I pushed him to do it. He was rightfully concerned about the traumatic effect this would have on David.

Bill asked the advice of a psychiatrist regarding weaning in this manner and was told to avoid it if possible. During this meeting, the psychiatrist gave Bill more insight into the difficult time I was going through. This helped tremendously. With his added emotional support, I dropped the idea of weaning and was able to pull myself together enough to avoid a breakdown.

"Having a baby can put a strain on a marriage. Having one with extreme fussiness can push the strongest marriages to the point of divorce. When there's an infant who's miserable for months, the parents' anger has to go some place and it's usually toward each other. Bill hated coming home. I counted the minutes till he got there, then raged at him when he arrived. It was fortunate that we had a strong marriage to begin with and Bill had the maturity to handle a wife who was an emotional wreck.

"During the winter, I was too depressed to take David out very much. To get dressed and take him for a short walk in the buggy took all my strength. Even during those short walks, I'd be terribly tense, waiting for him to start screaming.

"Unfortunately for us, the relatives and friends who could have helped me the most in caring for David live out of town. This was an added burden and made the winter endless.

"David's teething was also a complicating factor in his health. From the time he was six months until he was ten and one half months old he had from four to ten bowel movements a day. Each time he cut a tooth he would begin vomiting a week before and continued until he had the dry heaves on the day the tooth was cut. I can remember changing my clothes several times a day and holding him constantly.

"At ten and one half months, after David finally cut his eighth tooth, we saw a tremendous change in him. He soon began crawling (he never could before) and then at twelve months he began walking. He was so proud of himself and happy. For the first time, I could begin taking him out and enjoy it.

"A few days after he cut his teeth, he began eating solids—everything. This turned out to be a mixed blessing. It appeared that his stomach wasn't quite ready for them. At night and during his nap, he developed severe gas pains. He'd awaken every one and one half to two hours screaming. We could hear and smell the gas as he doubled up in pain. Sometimes it would take forty-five minutes to an hour to get him back to sleep. During the day, except for naps, he had much less gas. He probably walked it off. He was in constant motion.

"Obviously, waking up every two hours was incredibly difficult on me but initially, I didn't mind it much. At least I had a happy baby during the day. A happy baby! I began to think I was an okay mother after all.

"David quickly caught up to other babies his age in many areas and I hoped would soon catch up in all others. He was very shy and needed more socialization since he had been in the house so much when he was younger.

"David was still waking up every few hours. The lack of sleep was taking its toll on all of us. I continued blaming his teeth. I thought his molars might be coming in and upsetting his stomach. I convinced myself that once his teeth came in everything would be fine.

"In the meantime, I was still nursing him to sleep and nursing him every time he woke up. Bill and I almost never went out. My daytime schedule depended on when and if David was ready to nap. There were days he never did.

"What I didn't notice were the subtle and gradual changes in David. He was becoming more and more grouchy. He was especially miserable in the morning, and grew more frightened in social situations.

"When he was fifteen months old, David ran a high fever for several days from a viral infection. A week later he ran a high fever again as a reaction to the measles vaccine. We had to hold him and carry him a great deal. When he got well, all he wanted to do was to be carried. He had no interest in going outside or playing. He just wanted me to read to him.

"I took David to play group the week after his illnesses. We hadn't been with the group for a month because of his nap schedule. He screamed the entire time.

"I was appalled when I compared him with the other babies. They were younger than David but were far ahead of him developmentally. What was most upsetting was watching those babies sit, concentrate and play with toys. David never played with toys; he was constantly moving.

"I felt like I was kicked in the gut again. There was still something wrong with my baby. Was he hyperactive despite the Feingold diet? Was his behavior due to my mothering?

"Dr K suggested the Sleep Disorders Center when David was about thirteen months old, but it took me a few months to face the fact that I needed to call. I knew the clinic dealt with parent and child interaction as well as physical disorders and I was too afraid of being criticized. I had convinced myself that David would get better on his own. Bill was afraid the clinic would discover some serious neurological disorder, so he was also reluctant to go.

"We were incredibly fortunate that we finally went. First and foremost, we learned we had a normal baby whose past behavior and lack of social development was due to sleep deprivation, not hyperactivity. Second, we learned we were not alone in our responses to David. Many parents of babies who had extreme fussiness continue to respond to them as if they were still ill and tend to foster the poor sleep patterns.

"We learned that we had to let David cry it out so he could get the sleep he so desperately needed. This turned out to be easier than either Bill or I anticipated. But we needed to retrain ourselves before we could retrain David. The doctor gave instructions on every possible contingency, including what to do if David threw up.

"Armed with our instructions, double scotches, frozen pizzas, Haagen Daazs's chocolate ice cream and a few chocolate bars—we were ready for a long night—we put David in bed while he was still awake. Fifteen minutes later, he was asleep! He was only up twice that night for approximately five minutes each time. This was the baby who was up every one and half-hours! David's sleep patterns have backtracked occasionally if he is teething or ill, but his normal pattern now is to sleep through the night, and to take one nap a day.

"Now that David sleeps through the night, we have a rested, happy baby and also a rested, happy mother. Not until I was sleeping through the night did I realize what a toll the sleep deprivation had taken on myself as well as David. We are really a happy family for the first time."

If the change in David's behavior seems unbelievable, remember that this is a mother prone to dramatization. I can attest, however, that trained night crying can sometimes be stopped almost overnight, as it was in this case. Perhaps the child senses in the parents' calm resolve that they really mean business.

The following description from a thirty-three-year-old housewife was given to me six months after a single visit. She describes many of the changes in parental behavior that David's family found useful.

### Dan's Mother

"When Dan was born, we knew he was someone very special. From the moment of birth I felt he was quite different from his older brother, Brian. I had hoped one of these differences would be his sleep behavior since Brian slept at least four to six hours less per day than any of his peers. Well, his sleep patterns were different from Brian's all right. Unfortunately, they were worse.

"We noticed from the beginning that Dan had always been a very light sleeper, especially for an infant. He would awaken at the slightest sound or disruption. Dan slept through the night (ten hours) for the first time at about one and half months old. I was thrilled but I knew, based on experience with our first son, that this could be a fluke. It was. That was the only night he did it until he was over eleven months old! From then on, Dan got up every one to three hours each night.

"For the first several months, I nursed him each time he

woke thinking he may be hungry since he refused solids. Then we tried other responses; my husband going to him, walking with him, rocking him, even letting him cry. We set up the playpen in our bedroom and put Dan there because he was waking his brother, but Dan invariably awoke when my husband and I came to bed. So we moved his playpen to the family room (farthest from Brian's and our bedrooms). Some nights I would put him in his crib and other nights, when we decided to let him cry, he would go back to the playpen. We were concerned that Dan would wake Brian or vice versa.

"Needless to say, this was wreaking havoc with our lives. I was getting up as many as four to five times per night with Dan. John would get up with Brian if he awoke. On a number of occasions he also got up with Dan. We would both have to be up for the day after 6:00 A.M., when my husband went to work. My fatigue was intensified since I was breast-feeding.

"John and I were always tired. We very often retired as early as 8:00 or 8:30 P.M. to try to catch up on sleep. It didn't help much since we still weren't getting a long stretch of uninterrupted sleep. One advantage John had over me is that he could immediately fall back to sleep during the night. Most times it took me a good half-hour or more to get back to sleep. This really was frustrating and gave me even less sleep.

"John and I grew more and more irritable with each other and the children due to fatigue, little or no relaxed time together, and frustration at not being able to solve Dan's problem. Dan was also showing ill effects of his sleep pattern. We knew we had to do something.

"At every baby checkup I mentioned to his doctor that he wasn't sleeping well. At first we discussed it rather casually. I implied that it was not a serious problem. I tend to let things go almost too long before I complain. Then we got to the point where Dan's doctor felt something should be done. Dan was nearly eight months old, and our doctor was getting concerned not only for Dan but also for me. I had to avoid getting too run down, especially since I had two small children to take care of.

"Dr. H first prescribed Benadryl, an antihistamine, at bedtime. He said this should make Dan drowsy and better able to fall asleep. Nothing changed. We continued this for about a week. Dan has always been, and still is, most difficult when it comes to trying to get medicine, or even food, into him. Unless he can feed himself, he wants no part of it. It was a struggle every night, especially since I wasn't really comfortable giving my child medication when he wasn't sick.

"I called Dr. H again. He felt it was time to use a mild sedative, but he wanted to consult with a pediatrician. The pediatrician concurred with Dr. H's decision, which made me frightened and very upset. Dr. H prescribed Noctec (chloryl hydrate) at bedtime and during the night if Dan awakened. Both doctors insisted that this drug was not habit-forming. The idea was to get him into a deep enough sleep so that he would not wake as easily during the night.

"I was very uncomfortable with the situation, but that night we tried to get the dosage into Dan. He took about half of it. He did fall asleep quicker, but four hours later he woke and continued his pattern of waking every one or two hours through the rest of the night.

"The next day Dan caught a cold. It was my excuse to take him to see Dr. H in person again. He checked Dan out for any possible problems beyond a mild cold but Dan seemed fine.

"The doctor and I talked over my apprehensions about the sedative. I have always avoided medication or drugs if at all possible. Dr. H had seemed to have the same philosophy. I told the doctor that I felt I was being selfish by drugging my son so that I could get a night's sleep. He reassured me that we were doing this for Dan, that he needed sleep as much as I did. The doctor convinced me—sort of.

"For the next week or so we went back to giving Dan Benadryl in a normal dosage for his cold. As soon as he was healthy again we resumed using the Noctec. It still did no good. Dan would sort of pass out right after he took the medication but then revert to his old pattern after four hours or so. At his nine-month checkup, Dr. H doubled the dosage. We continued this for ten days, and then gave up. We were about to schedule an appointment with a pediatric neurologist when a close friend saw a special report on the evening news about children's sleeping problems. From the information I received on the phone and the questionnaire I received, I felt that this, rather than the pediatric neurologist, was the correct next step for Dan.

"Dan was over eleven months old when my husband and I took him to see Dr. Weissbluth. We were very nervous about what he would find, but deep inside I knew there was nothing really wrong with Dan; that he really was normal. When the doctor arrived, Dan seemed content, so we went over our questionnaire; answered further questions from the doctor who discussed our thoughts while Dr. W observed Dan.

"The doctor examined him and told us that there was nothing wrong with Dan. Naturally, our response was, 'Great, but why won't he sleep normally? Does he just require very little sleep?' We were told that a child Dan's age needs ten to twelve hours of sleep at night plus one to four hours during the day.

"Dr. W said that Dan seemed to be extremely sensitive to all stimuli and suggested we do the following: take Brian out of the room—his tossing and even his breathing were probably disturbing Dan. Keep Dan's room as dark as possible— take out the nightlight; mount a room darkening shade on the outside of the window frame to block out even the light along the edges, and of course, keep the door closed. Take all toys out of his bed and have Dan sleep in a sleeper so that only his hands and head were exposed to rubbing against the sheets. Do no 'noisy' cleaning and turn off phones while Dan slept.

"If Dan still woke up during the night, we were not to go to him. I was concerned that maybe Dan was waking due to hunger. Dr. W said that Dan was the correct height and weight for his age and was not waking because of hunger.

"He warned us that Dan could possibly cry as long as five and one half hours the first night. Before I could verbalize my thoughts, Dr. W stated them for me. He said that, since I wouldn't be able to sleep anyway, I should get up and do something such as take a ride, read a book, watch TV, whatever. Let my husband handle the situation. This crying would stop within five to seven days.

"Fortunately, we did not need to experience any of this trauma. We did all that Dr. W suggested to minimize any stimuli for Dan during the night. We had only two bedrooms so poor Brian was put to bed in our room and moved to a sofa-bed in the family room when we retired. The situation was obviously far from ideal, but it worked.

"Dan slept ten and a half hours straight that first night. I was so exhausted that I slept through also. When I woke at 5:00 A.M., I wanted to run in and see if Dan was still alive!

"It has been almost six months since then and Dan has slept through every night. Occasionally he will wake during the night and cry or call out but we don't go to him and he goes back to sleep shortly.

"After about two months we decided we should try putting Brian back in his own room. Poor Brian had gone through a lot because of Dan's problems; not only was he expected to keep very quiet when Dan was napping, but he couldn't even sleep in his own bed!

"The problem was that Dan needed complete darkness with the door closed, while Brian required a nightlight and the door open. It took a while but they both got used to having the door open with the nightlight in the bathroom out of Dan's view. Dan was in the relative darkness but Brian could see some light from his bed. We put Dan to bed with the door closed. Brian goes to bed after Dan falls asleep and after that the door stays open for the night.

"Dan has his toys back in his bed since he's older and will now play with them for a while in the morning. He's still a very light sleeper and we've had to adjust, but things are very good around here now. We haven't had a group of people over after Dan's bedtime and we don't keep Dan out past 7:30 or 8:00 P.M. because we want him to fall asleep in his bed for the night. We used to be able to put Brian to sleep at someone else's house and just take him home to his own bed relatively undisturbed. That would be impossible for Dan. We don't leave the house if it's close to naptime and we get home quickly if we are already out.

"All of these changes have been inconvenient, but well worth the trouble. Things will get even better than they already are. We're having a couple of bedrooms put in upstairs so this will remove Dan further from the first-floor commotion.

"It's amazing what a sleep problem' can do to a family. Dan's problem seemed to totally consume our lives. Besides the physical effects to us all through fatigue, it took its toll on our social life as well. We rarely went out in the evening or had people over to our home. We seldom had time to just spend with each other. We were preoccupied, and too darned tired. We were lucky to make it through the day!

"Needless to say, our lives have improved dramatically. We are especially happy that it took no drugs or medication and that nothing is wrong with our son.

"I personally received an added good feeling from all of this. I belong to a parenting support group and the word passed rather quickly that one of my children had a sleep problem that was solved. I have received many calls from mothers who are experiencing trouble with their child's sleep pattern and now I can confidently steer them in the right direction to get help."

Another mother of a very stimulus-sensitive baby was told by her pediatrician to make her baby's bedroom "like a cave." Unfortunately he provided no specific information on how to do this.

The mother, a thirty-year-old artist, wondered if he meant she was supposed to paint stalactites, stalagmites, and bats on the walls! Her comments, below, illustrate how dramatic improvement can occur rapidly, and how important it is for both parents to make careful plans about letting baby alone.

### Jackie's Mother

"Everywhere I went people smiled at my baby, Jackie, because she lights up for everyone. People were amazed at how happy she always appeared and how well she behaved. I'd graciously acknowledge their praises but at the same time I'd think to myself: Yeah, but if she would only sleep through the night, or even a little during the day!'

"As an infant, Jackie was breastfed, adapted well to any schedule and to my amazement slept through the night. In fact, I remember bragging about it to all my friends who were now mothers and walked around like zombies from exhaustion. Well, my sleep-filled nights were short-lived.

"When Jackie was three months old her sleep habits turned into a nightmare. During the day she took two or three naps which lasted about fifteen minutes apiece. She would stay up until 10:30 P.M., wake up five to eight times for a bottle or a diaper change or a half-hour of attention. Usually she would go right back to sleep and get up for good at 6:00 or 7:00.

"We were so desperate that we took any advice that was offered. We added cereal to her formula, started early on solids, fed her chamomile tea, eliminated naps in the afternoon, bathed her at night for an hour, gave her massages, took her swimming and then tried the most painful experiment of all: we let her cry for half-hour periods at night before giving her a bottle. We did this for eight straight days with no results. Then for the next two days we let her cry for forty-five minutes at a time. We gave up.

"I hired someone to live in and help me attend to Jackie at night since after two months of interrupted sleep I was unable to function. When Jackie turned eight months, my pediatrician recommended that she take an amino acid with dinner that would act as a sedative. This made me stop and think. I opted for a consultation with Dr. Weissbluth.

"While I was talking with him, Jackie performed one of her fifteen minute naps in her stroller. It was apparent to Dr.

Weissbluth that when she awoke she was still very tired. She was living on nervous energy, he said. He pointed out that all babies need about fourteen hours of sleep, so my conclusion that 'Jackie just didn't need that much sleep' was a false notion.

"I mentioned that her father would come home late from work, tip-toe into her room and she would snap out of her sleep immediately to play with him. Jackie always seemed sensitive to noise. A moderately loud sound would make her jump, and if she were sleeping the slightest sound would wake her up.

"Dr. Weissbluth suggested that Jackie's sensitivity to stimuli was the root of her sleeping problems. He said she should sleep in a pitch dark, quiet atmosphere. He said I shouldn't respond to her crying for attention at night as long as she was healthy. He also said I would most likely be up all night the first night and that after three nights it would definitely subside. He said my husband would have to support me in carrying out this plan; that was my main worry.

"When I got home I immediately took Jackie's crib into our den, which has no windows. I put her down for a nap and within two minutes she was sound asleep! She slept for two hours! I was sure the covers were over her head and she was suffocating to death, or that she had jumped out of her crib and was passed out on the floor, but I didn't dare go peek. Jackie woke up smiling, ready to play. I couldn't believe it.

"I explained everything to my husband. He wasn't very convinced that we should just let her cry. I called up a friend of a friend who had had a similar problem with her baby and was claiming that Dr. W's treatment worked. I wanted her to tell my husband of her great results. That finally sold him, so we got set to try it.

"My husband slept at the new house we were building, my housekeeper locked herself in her bedroom and I sat up working in the kitchen, prepared to be up all night.

"We put Jackie down to sleep in the den at 8:00 P.M. She cried for forty minutes and then went to sleep. I worked in the kitchen until 1:30 when it dawned on me that maybe she

)e up crying all night after all. I heard her
) but she didn't cry until 8:45 the next morn-
ing. Three days later she still slept straight through the night
from 8:00 P.M. until 7:00 A.M. and took two naps, one from
10:00 to 11:30 A.M., and another from 1:30 to 2:00 P.M.
We've all been celebrating ever since."

As these testimonies indicate, older children who do not
sleep through the night grind their parents down. It's a long
nightmare. These cures may sound miraculous, but I assure
you, when the baby and the parents are really ready, their
joint bad habit can be broken just this quickly. So please, do
not be afraid to leave your children alone at night. You are
teaching a health habit: prolonged and uninterrupted sleep
. . . for your child and yourselves!

### What Should I Do?

Dear parents, when your baby is crying, do nothing.
But do nothing deliberately, quietly, gently, confidently and
firmly. In other words, please try to develop an attitude of:

Purposeful inattention
Studied inattentiveness
Gentle firmness
Constructive resignation
Expectant observation
Watchful waiting

Be attentive to your baby's behavior at night, but try to
cultivate a detached and relaxed attitude. As you have read,
it does work!

# 13

## Love Your Baby

Every baby is a unique person. Even identical twins have subtle differences. But all babies have certain instincts, which might have survival value such as the rooting reflex. Fussing/crying might also be based on a survival reflex: a signal system based on sometimes being apart from mother, a separation signal. The signal communicates, "Come to me, pick me up, feed me." But the signaling system may be imperfectly attuned to the reality that while the baby is in fact held in mother's arms and at the breast, the baby has some expectation of being inside the womb. It's a little like saying that the system was designed for a twelve month gestation and has difficulty coping with the bombardment of extra external stimulation resulting from being born at nine months gestation. You can see how confusing this would be for a newborn!

There is no reason to introduce psychological terms such as 'fear', 'loneliness', 'tension', or 'anxiety.' These terms simply cause us to feel that we are bad parents if our child cries because our baby has 'unmet psychological needs.'

If your newborn fusses or cries despite your best efforts, always remember:

## IT'S NOT YOUR FAULT

Some newborns cry a little, some cry a lot. Each day may be different for each baby. During the first few months, nothing about your baby—including crying—will be predictable. At times you may feel thoroughly bewildered.

Relax. After three or four months, things usually calm down. You have read about babies who created havoc in their parents' lives and then developed into sweet little four- and five-month olds. If you accept your fussy baby as a dear, wonderful child who will outgrow the fussing/crying phase, you will be more relaxed and better prepared to cope with the challenges each day brings.

If your very young baby cries more than three hours most days, if you don't seem to be able to console him, and if this has been going on for several weeks, it may help you to think of him as having a very common, blessedly short-lived condition called 'extreme fussiness.' I hope you understand more about extreme fussiness after reading this book.

Do not expect that finding a name for your child's behavior will end your bewilderment. Extreme fussiness changes from day to day. During the time they suffer from extreme fussiness spells, infants may also be erratic in sleeping patterns, irregular in the degree to which they can be consoled, and show great variability in how much they cry. Parents tend to think of extreme fussiness as constant state, but I think that in retrospect they focus on the worst nights and let everything blur together. Extreme fussiness is not as regular or relentless, as it may seem.

It will help you and your baby if you can emphasize the good, quiet, calm times. Do not let the 10 percent or 25 percent of your baby's day when she is extremely fussy overshadow the rest.

You may assume, like many people, that your own anxieties are transmitted to your infant and cause him to cry or fuss or sleep poorly. I urge you to put this idea out of your mind. Researchers now know that powerful and complex biologic forces contribute to each baby's behavior, including his fussing/crying and sleeping patterns. There are many factors which neither you nor your pediatrician can influence. So the best advice may be as simple as this: be patient and loving during the many difficult hours of the first few months, and don't be afraid to try a few of the techniques that have proven effective for others. It is especially important for fathers to get involved as early as possible: infant massage, walks, car rides, and feeding their newborns.

Remember that unexplained crying occurs in all infants during the first few months of life. In only about 20 percent does it become severe enough to be called extreme fussiness. Despite much conjecture, there has been a striking failure to discover any definite gastrointestinal, allergic, or maternally provoked causes of extreme fussiness. It may be set off instead by one or more physiologic disturbances.

What these physiological causes might be is a question for further study. As I have suggested, they might include disordered regulation of breathing, sleeping patterns which are out of sync with other body rhythms, or abnormal levels of naturally occurring substances such as melatonin, prostaglandins or progesterone.

There is a great deal that we do not know about a baby's hormones and chemicals, the developing brain, the effects of low birth weight, the control over vital functions during sleep and the biological basis for rhythmic patterns. Associations among measurable temperament, sleep patterns, breathing during sleep, and crying suggest that extreme fussiness may be related to all four. Most likely, extreme fussiness is the common, final pathway of several related or unrelated disturbances. Solving this mystery will take the work of experts in many fields. Much more cooperative research is needed by the "larks" who observe awake behavior, the "owls" who observe sleeping patterns, and the "hawks" who provoke, prod, and challenge our babies to respond.

Throughout this book I have emphasized that gradations occur in all our measurements: duration of crying spells, sleep durations, temperament ratings, melatonin and progesterone levels and respiratory pauses during sleep. Is it really necessary to impose labels like 'extreme fussiness/colic' and 'Difficult' Temperaments? Researchers, in order to study, divide behavior into categories like normal and abnormal, easy and difficult, or extreme fussiness and no extreme fussiness. You as parents should always be thinking of that little person—not a condition, a ranking, or a label.

When your baby cries at night, remember the smiling, cheerful moments. Focus on everything lovely about her while you help her work out her difficulties.

### Hugs, Kisses and Love Help Your Baby Grow

After a few months of age, helping your baby learn to sleep after the fussiness quiets down is very important. Regularity of handling, feeding, and sleeping calms down the storm of newborn fussiness. Do not become a slave to your baby's sleep schedule; instead, respect his need to have good quality sleep in the same way you later will be sensitive to good quality nutrition. Try to distinguish between routine days and exceptional days. On routine days, somewhat organize your activities around naps and an early bedtime. On exceptional days, sleep may suffer because of special events.

### My Sons

Since my firstborn son's extremely fussy days (and nights!), researchers have learned much about infant behaviors. Would I handle my first son, who had extreme fussiness, or my second, third, or fourth sons, who did not have extreme fussiness, any differently now? Absolutely not. The natural course of parenting hasn't changed significantly because of scientific endeavors. I play with my children and I am tickled when they laugh. I smile when they giggle and I am distressed when they cry. I feel how my children feel and I share their joys and sorrows. I want to love, hug, kiss, caress, tease and wrestle with my children. Loving hugs and kisses still are the best treatment for developing an affectionate, giving personality.

Your baby is very special. Each baby is a miracle. Accept and love your bundle of joy with all your heart and all your soul, and be assured that soon your newborn will become that what we all hope for, a sweet baby.